CHOICES

Real People Share Their Stories of How They Overcame the Challenges to Design a Better Life

Carol McManus • Alan Skidmore

New York, New York

Published by
CKC Global Publishing
301 E 57th Street, 4th fl
New York, NY 10022

Copyright © 2017 by Carol McManus and Alan Skidmore

All rights reserved. No part of this book may be reproduced or transmitted in any form or by in any means, electronic or mechanical, including photocopying, recording, or by any information storage and retrieval system, without the written permission of the Publisher, except where permitted by law.

Manufactured in the United States of America, or in the United Kingdom when distributed elsewhere.

McManus, Carol and Skidmore, Alan
      Choices: Real People Share Their Stories of How They
      Overcame Challenges to Design a Better Life
      LCCN: 2017951466
      ISBN: 978-1-938015-82-3
      eBook: 978-1-938015-83-0

Cover design: Joe Potter
Interior design: Claudia Volkman
Carol McManus photo: Matthew Abourezk
Alan Skidmore photo: Yoti Telio

ACKNOWLEDGMENTS

This book is dedicated to our spouses, Kevin and Penny. They supported us throughout the process and never wavered in their commitment to our vision.

We want to thank our contributors, without whom this book would not exist. They were the inspiration to uncovering the importance of making choices in our lives. Through their stories, we unlocked the key to understanding the enormous role that values play in everything we do, say, or become.

It is with heartfelt appreciation that we acknowledge all the people in our lives who individually and collectively inspired us over the years to be able to write this book. They include our teachers, our spiritual leaders, our friends, our family, and our business associates. There would be no adequate way to name all of them, but each one of them played an important role, and for that, we are deeply grateful.

Alan would specifically like to thank his wife, Penny, and his sons, Justin and Jesse, for the joy and happiness they have brought to his life. Also to his parents, Lambert and Reba Skidmore, for their love and support while giving him the solid foundation to help make better choices over the years.

Carol would specifically like to thank her husband, Kevin, for all his patience and for being a consistent role model of what values mean in life. And a special prayer for her mother and father whose unwavering guidance and encouragement put her on a lifelong path to achievement. Those lessons taught so many years ago led to the ability to make difficult choices and face whatever came her way.

And our thank you would not be complete without acknowledging our publisher, Karen Strauss, our copyeditor, Claudia Volkman, and our cover designer, Joe Potter. They brought our words and vision to life.

PRAISE FOR *CHOICES*

"OMG! Finding this book is like finding the Holy Grail! It's actually a User's Guide for life! Carol and Alan intelligently discuss everything from Business to Career, Education to Environment, Health and Money Matters, Relationships and Marriage, to Self-Discovery and Spirituality. I always wondered why we never came with a User's Guide . . . Now I've found it! *Choices* is a MUST-READ!"

LON SAFKO, AUTHOR OF *THE SOCIAL MEDIA BIBLE*
AND *THE FUSION MARKETING BIBLE*
lonsafko.com

"A must-read for anyone at any age or stage of life! Choices has arrived at the perfect time. In today's fast-paced, wired world, understanding why we make certain decisions will help shape the future of our lives. Easy to read, and the stories are inspiring, illuminating, and encouraging. Thank you, Alan and Carol, for this wise and valuable resource!"

JOY CHUDACOFF, FOUNDER/CEO SMART WOMEN SMART SOLUTIONS®
smartwomensolutions.com

"Life is about 'choices.' In *Choices*, longtime business advocates and consultants Carol McManus and Alan Skidmore explain that choices have consequences, and consequences affect those around us and impact us for the rest of our lives. We live in an age where many don't want to take responsibility for their actions and choices, but Carol and Alan show us how to get 'in touch' with our values and take time to process life choices in a different way, one that will bring the results we are looking for.

"This book covers how community, fairness, loyalty, responsibility, and self-respect can help us reach our goals and asks the tough questions when it comes to career growth, relationships, and the curveballs life constantly throws at us. Ultimately 'life' is a choice for many, and *Choices* is the perfect resource to keep at our side in this fast-paced world."

RICK LIMPERT, AUTHOR, BROADCASTER AND SPORTS TECH WRITER
ricklimpert.squarespace.com

PRAISE FOR *CHOICES*

"*Choices* is filled with meaningful and compelling stories. It is thoroughly researched and well written. Most of all, it shares great insights from two successful professionals who have succinctly organized and structured a discussion of life's major choices. In the end, it guides you to make better, more thoughtful choices and be more successful in your life and work. Well done!"

DOUG CAMPBELL, THE "SUCCESS COACH" AND AUTHOR OF *WHERE TO GO FROM HERE: REINVENTING YOUR BUSINESS AND YOUR CAREER*
thesuccesscoach.com

"Truth IS stranger than fiction. As a fiction author and an English professor teaching fiction, I engage every day with young (and older) adults who are at sea with their values and struggle with making choices. This provocative and truthful book provides new insights and solutions for dealing with life's challenges. A brilliant piece of work that blends humor, wisdom, and personal introspection. Required reading for anyone who wants to redesign their life."

GARY (GOSHGARIAN, PHD) BRAVER, BEST-SELLING AND AWARD-WINNING AUTHOR OF *TUNNEL VISION* AND PROFESSOR OF ENGLISH, NORTHEASTERN UNIVERSITY
garybraver.com

"Every day we make both large and small choices. And many times, it's the small choices that come back to bite us. Through their own experiences, and interviews with amazing people, Carol McManus and Alan Skidmore cover all aspects of life and the types of choices we make. If you feel it's time to make better choices, I highly suggest you read this book."

CRAIG DUSWALT, SPEAKER, AUTHOR, PODCASTER, AND CREATOR OF THE BRANDS ROCKSTAR MARKETING AND ROCK YOUR LIFE
craigduswalt.com

PRAISE FOR *CHOICES*

"Carol's and Alan's book is jam-packed with life lessons covering every topic a human being needs to consider, from business opportunities to managing ourselves and our homes. The CHOICES underlying everything we do are illustrated here in memorable and applicable ways. Its subtitle could've been *A Life Primer*—that's how helpful it is."

JANE POLLAK, BUSINESS COACH, SPEAKER, ARTIST, AND AUTHOR OF
SOUL PROPRIETOR: 101 LESSONS FROM A LIFESTYLE ENTREPRENEUR IN 2001
janepollak.com

"Sprinkled with touching moments of courage and wisdom, these stories help us recognize the importance not only of our choices, but the need to choose. Carol and Alan challenge us to explore how and why we act, using lessons from real people in situations that illustrate how critical it is to shape our lives, one little decision at a time."

MATTHEW FERRARA, PHILOSOPHER, SPEAKER, PHOTOGRAPHER
matthewferrara.com

"A phrase I often share in keynote presentations and on *The Live It Forward Show* podcast is this: 'The choices you make . . . make you.' This isn't just a catchy statement; it's true. The choices we make determine our direction, and direction determines destiny. Carol and Alan's book shares story after story about the power of choices in real people's lives. If you are someone who wants to make better and wiser choices, read this book!"

KENT JULIAN, KEYNOTE SPEAKER, CONSULTANT,
HOST OF *THE LIVE IT FORWARD SHOW*
liveitforward.com

PRAISE FOR *CHOICES*

"As we all work to build amazing businesses or have a larger impact through social programs, occasionally we need to step back and evaluate what got here. *Choices* is a book that both inspires you to move forward with purpose while also encouraging you to look back at the path that lead you to today. Carol and Alan do a fantastic job of weaving in personal and often thought provoking stories with matter of fact actionable content. Books like this push me to want to be better."

**JABEZ LEBRET, CHIEF OF SCHOOLS SISU ACADEMY,
CONTRIBUTOR TO *FORBES***
jabezlebret.com

"Having made tough choices throughout my life, I can attest it is our core values that steer our lives toward one of significance. This book amazingly covers all aspects of life and the types of choices we make. If you are wanting to make better choices that lead to a better life, read this book!"

**LARRY BROUGHTON, AWARD-WINNING ENTREPRENEUR AND CEO,
BEST-SELLING AUTHOR, TV PERSONALITY**
larrybroughton.me

*Every strike brings me closer
to the next home run.*
BABE RUTH

CONTENTS

Introduction 1
Why Choices Matter 3

PART ONE
Business 11
Career and Work 27
Education 37
Environment 47
Family and Friends 51
Health 65
Money Matters 71
Personal 83
Relationships and Marriage 95
Scarcity vs. Abundance 111
Self-Discovery 119
Spirituality 129
Suicide 137
When Disaster Strikes 147

PART TWO
First Major Choices 155
Regional Influences 167
Values 173
Evaluating Choices 183
Last Thoughts 187

Credits 189
Recommended Resources 191
About the Authors 196

INTRODUCTION

*The way to get started is to
quit talking and begin doing.*
WALT DISNEY

DID YOU EVER think about the fact that everything we do in our lives is about making choices? Let's start with the little ones. When you get up in the morning, you make a choice about what you're going to wear that day. When you go to the kitchen, you make a choice about what you're going to have for breakfast. Is it going to be oatmeal? Bacon and eggs? Toast? Or just a cup of coffee? And on your way to work, you decide how you're going to get there—what route are you going to take? What will get you there in the fastest time? Which one will take you past your favorite coffee establishment? And when you pull into Starbucks or Dunkin Donuts or the local joint, will it be decaf, regular coffee, or maybe a fancy latte?

What are the consequences of all these choices?

The truth is that consequences are the result of every single choice we make. Sometimes the consequences are good, and sometimes the consequences are bad. The bigger question is: Can you anticipate what the outcome is going to be and are you making the right choices in life?

The topics in this book are varied; they cover the key aspects of life every one of us face at some point. Our goal is to open conversation around these topics. Any topic may spark your desire to do more research of your own and stimulate new conversations.

Our intention is not to lecture or judge . . . our approach is to share our own insights and perspectives along with personal stories from real people—not celebrities or star athletes or high-profile politicians, but folks like us—who have made difficult choices in their lives that had lasting and far-reaching effects. You will learn what led up to those choices, what happened as a result, and what personal values influenced them along the way. Some choices were made a long time ago and others more recently. The people we interviewed for this book range in age from eighteen to eighty-nine. We want to thank every one of our contributors. In most cases, we have changed their identity to protect their privacy, but every story is factual and from the heart.

We can all learn from each other's choices. If you would like to have better outcomes in life, then starting today, we can help *you* look at your choices in a different way. By reading this book, we are giving you some new tools to make better choices for yourself, for your family, and for your future.

WHY CHOICES MATTER

Your beliefs become your thoughts,
Your thoughts become your words,
Your words become your actions,
Your actions become your habits,
Your habits become your values,
Your values become your destiny.
MAHATMA GANDHI

ARE CHOICES AND decisions the same? What are the true definitions? The definition of *choice*, according to Merriam-Webster, is "the act of choosing." The definition of *decision* is "the act or process of deciding" or "a determination arrived at after consideration." And according to *Roget's 21st Century Thesaurus*, each word is offered as an alternative for the other. For that reason, in this book, we're going to use *choice* and *decision* as one and the same.

What are the differences between the choices we make today versus those of our grandparents? It's been said that today we make more choices in one day than our grandparents made in two months. For example, we are continuously bombarded with multiple messages of advertising: where to buy, who to buy from, does it really work, what are the side effects, who to follow, and the list goes on. Advertising used to be limited to radio, television, and print, with billboards and park benches thrown in for good measure. Now we have added the Internet, social media, text messaging, email, apps, and telemarketing. Each form of advertising contributes to our confusion and frustration in making even the simplest of everyday choices. Every advertiser is competing for eyeballs and the plastic in your wallet.

Let's look at a typical day. What should I wear today? Where am I going to eat? What route to work should I take? Is it going to rain today? If it rains, do I take an umbrella? For city dwellers, do I take the train, subway, bus, taxi, or ferry? Or maybe my best option is Uber or Lyft. Do I even go to work today, or should I just stay home? If I stay home, do I have enough vacation days? I should go to work because I have a meeting on the calendar. What am I supposed to bring? Am I really interested in this? I really need to finish this other project. I have a plethora of other things to do—my desk phone is ringing, my mobile phone is ringing, I have three text messages, two Skype requests, four pings from Messenger, and 175 emails in my inbox. I want to get to zero before the end of the day, but that's probably not going to happen.

Catch the anxiety?

Think of the compound effect in just one week impacting all the choices you don't get to and move to the *tomorrow* list. It's no wonder products like Tums, Pepcid, Zantac, and Rolaids continue to fly off the shelves. You might think that facing a horde of daily choices would make us stronger, better equipped to handle the big choices in life, but the opposite may be true. Perhaps the crush of choices you are expected to make has driven you to make fast, sometimes rash choices, or perhaps you are so paralyzed by the weight of making choices that you avoid them at all costs.

The cycle goes on and on and on. You know exactly what we're talking about. We are so overwhelmed with the number of decisions we are saddled with every day that we just freeze up. It gets frustrating!

Fifty years ago, it was a simpler time, especially from a technology standpoint. There was no technology in our homes or cars, or Velcroed to the palm of our hands. Think to an even earlier time when our grandparents and great-grandparents were focused on food, shelter, and providing for the family. One hundred years ago in the United States, we were just getting electricity distributed throughout the country. The telephone was an invention that existed only in certain places. Commercial air travel was in its infancy and inaccessible to most people. If you traveled any real distance, you were likely to use the train. If you couldn't afford a horseless carriage, you probably used a bicycle or the reliable horse and buggy.

It is also interesting to reflect on how the *speed* of technology has changed over the past hundred years and how that has affected our lives and our choices.

Reflections by Alan:

My wife and I recently watched the British TV series *Downton Abbey*. It was one of the best shows we've ever seen. The story was based in the period between 1912 to 1926 in the United Kingdom. It focused on an aristocratic family and all the intricacies of their lives. Major events during that time, such as World War I and the sinking of the Titanic, were incorporated in the scripts to demonstrate how society viewed things at the time. What was particularly curious to me, being an engineer, was the story of bringing electricity to the castle for the first time. They really didn't know what to think about it. When they brought a telephone to the castle, the reaction was, "Eh, who needs this?" And when a radio was introduced by Rose, it was met with mixed reactions. As I recall, the Earl of Grantham fumed, "I don't want a radio in here. We do not need that kind of thing! We can learn everything from newspapers."

But technology has rocketed change. I find it funny because now we are bombarded with so many different options: Internet radio, Pandora, Spotify, iHeart, GooglePlay—all new means of communication that didn't exist before 1993. Now we have satellite radio in our cars and satellite television with nearly a thousand different channels. There are so many different choices to make versus one hundred years ago. Our world today is much more complicated than it was in the past. That doesn't make it better, but it doesn't necessarily make it worse either; it's just different and we learn to deal with it. Depending on your age and technical savvy, each new challenge may seem like a steep hill to climb.

The truth of the matter is that, whether someone lived one hundred years ago, two hundred years ago, or lives now, we are all still human beings struggling to meet our basic needs and fulfill our dreams. We all want to be loved. We want to be included. We want to be involved. We want to feel like we have a purpose. We want to know that our lives have meaning, that we can make a difference, and maybe, just maybe, that we will be remembered long after our time ends.

I believe those basic human needs, no matter where you live or how old you are, will always remain at the core of what drives our choices along with our values. The common factor surrounding the choices we make ties back to relationships with family, friends, work, and ultimately ourselves—and ultimately to hopefully live a good and positive life.

Reflections by Carol:

One of my memories from important conversations with my father centered around his advice, "I don't care what you choose to do with your life. I just want to make sure you are happy and can always support yourself."

It's easy to understand why a father would want his only child to be happy. What might seem a bit curious is his concern that I always be able to support myself. If you know a little more about him, it's easier to understand. My father was born in 1907 and as a young man worked on Wall Street in the time leading up to the Great Depression. Fortunately, he left that work for a new career before the Crash, but like all Americans, he was deeply impacted by the economic climate during that time.

His entire life was built around making conservative choices that would not put himself or his family at risk. He was also practical and realized that whether you are a man or a woman, you should not depend on anyone else for your financial security. Hence, the advice.

It wasn't until recently, while I was writing this book, that I realized every critical choice I've made in my life was grounded in that sage advice. I have been married twice, but I've never depended on either husband for my financial security. The education and experience I've acquired over the years has been with an eye to independence and financial success.

I have made deliberate choices in all aspects of my life that centered around being able to support myself no matter what. Perhaps that it why I am so vocal, so opinionated, and so passionate about helping others discover their true potential. It's my dream for everyone to enjoy the same self-reliance, self-determination, and freedom to realize anything they set out to achieve.

I would like to think that I've made more good choices than bad choices in life. It is true that the lessons we remember, the ones that stick with us for life, often come from the bad choices. However, I believe the same lessons can be learned from good choices. Life is too short to second-guess ourselves. If you take the approach that every choice is a good choice because it was the right one at the time, then you can let go of the guilt, the remorse, and the heartbreak for choices that took a bad turn.

My philosophy about choices is quite simple really. If you make a choice and you're not happy with the outcome, then make a new choice. But no matter what, keep moving forward. Keep exercising your power to choose!

You are who you are today as a result of all your previous choices. If you stop and think about it, where you stand today, right this minute, right this second, is where you landed because of all the choices you made in your life, leading up to this moment. Were your choices good or bad, profitable, healthy, or spiritual? Would you wish for a do-over for some of the choices you made?

Perhaps you felt you had no control over some choices; maybe those choices were made for you. And it's possible that you made choices based on faulty information or shameful influence.

Take a quick self-test to gauge whether choices you made were yours or directed by others:

- Did you go to college?
- What school did you attend?
- Why did you pick that school?
- How did you choose your major?
- What was your first job out of college?

You get the idea. Chances are these decisions were heavily influenced by your parents or your school counselors. After all, isn't that their role—to guide us along the way until they are confident we can make our own choices?

Perhaps, but the real responsibility of parents, schools, and religious institutions is to equip children with the skills needed to make their own choices by the time they reach maturity. In this country, that is eighteen years old. At what age were you allowed to make important life choices for yourself?

Let's keep the time clock moving forward. Why did you marry the person you did? Why did you not marry your first girlfriend or your second boyfriend? Why did you decide to have kids . . . or not?

Every milestone in life is a great time to reflect on the choices that got us there. Why did you do what you did? What information did you have available to you at the time? Who influenced your decision? Were there other choices open to you?

We believe that choices are not necessarily good or bad—they are just choices. The exception to this thinking are choices that violate the law, ethics, and morality. For example, if you make a choice to kill someone, take your own life, or steal from others, we can agree that those are pretty bad choices.

But what if your family was starving and you were out of work—would stealing to feed your family be a bad choice or an act of desperation? Is it an example of moral lapse or the choice to survive another day? These kinds of deep questions are perhaps unnecessary in the grand scheme of things. The point is simply that choices are often driven by circumstances and the judgment of good or bad then takes on new meaning.

Let's take a lighter approach to this subject. Have you ever been around someone who simply could *not* make up their mind? They could not and would not make a choice. Frustrating, isn't it?

Imagine yourself out to lunch with a group of colleagues from work. You agree to go to a local fast-food restaurant. One person, we'll call him Joe, cannot make up his mind about what to get for lunch. Now, in most fast-food establishments, there are maybe a dozen choices on the menu, and they rarely change. So what happens when Joe stares at the board for a full ten minutes agonizing over the options while half the group was waiting behind him in line and the ones who went first have already finished their lunch? Wow! It happens, and you can bet that Joe has the same difficulty with every choice he faces. If you're like Joe or you know someone who is, how far can you go in life if you can't make a decision because you're afraid you're going to be wrong?

That's the interesting thing about choices. There is no handbook that will give you the definitive answer to making the right choices. It is simply required that you *make one!*

There are times that you are going to make wrong decisions, but that doesn't mean you have failed. The more you fail, the more likely you are to succeed. But you need to at least try! Get out there. If you fall down, get back up. If you fall down seven times, get up eight.

You are going to make mistakes, so don't be worried about making mistakes. Obviously, try not to do anything stupid. We're not saying jump off the Empire State Building because you think you can fly. But when it comes to choices in business and life, make your choices based on the information you have at the time. Make a choice and do something. Don't just stand there. Move!

If you stand there long enough, I promise you, the train will run over you even if you are on the right track.

Making choices is not an easy process, and it doesn't get easier as you age. But making a radical choice can be life-affirming. Don't wait for someone to ask you, "What do you want?" Take out a piece of paper and write that question down at least eight times. Each time you answer, build on the answer that came before. You will find your true passion and you *will* make the right choice.

PART ONE

BUSINESS

Success is not final;
Failure is not fatal;
It is the courage to continue that counts.
Winston W. Churchill

IT'S FAIR TO say that business in the twenty-first century is struggling with how to attract, nurture, and retain customers. Competition is more fierce than ever, and old advertising messaging practices no longer work. The customer is in control of the information. All you need to do is look at sites like Yelp, Angie's List, Home Advisor, Foursquare, Glassdoor, or Manta; instead of letting your fingers do the walking in the Yellow Pages or asking a neighbor for a recommendation, we now turn to the Internet.

When we are looking for a book to read, the importance of *New York Times* book reviews pales in comparison to the reviews you find on Amazon. Consumer Reports continues to do thorough testing and publishes their findings in their monthly magazine, but we still look to the product reviews on Shopify, Trustpilot, and Google.

And of course, the influence of raves and rants on Facebook and Twitter are legendary. Just talk to the folks at United Airlines. Over the past several years, they have lost millions in revenue and driven away passengers because of experiences that were captured and shared through social media.

Jeffrey Gitomer, a well-known author, speaker, and business trainer, says businesses to succeed must move beyond customer satisfaction. It is about customer loyalty. "You don't earn loyalty in a day. You earn loyalty day-by-day." Some customers will stick with a company forever because they just love the company, the products, and the way they are treated. But when the trust is broken and they begin to feel like a commodity rather than a valued customer, they will look elsewhere to take their business.

You may be wondering what this has to do with choices. It's simple really. This chapter is about choices we make that affect our companies. Whether you are a one-man or one-woman enterprise, a small business or a large corporation, every choice you make has an impact on your customer. Do you stop to think about how a decision reflects your business' values? Do you assess the potential negative impact on your customer or merely calculate the upside potential?

Reflections by Alan:

I have been using a bank in town for the past ten years or so. I use it for our personal checking, business checking, savings, and so on. They are convenient, the staff is courteous and efficient, and their interest rates are competitive. So far so good, but I have kind of come to the conclusion that just about all banks are the same. They all provide checking, savings, mortgages, and all the other good stuff you might need from a bank.

Because of technology, we really do not have to physically go to the bank much anymore. We can do direct deposit. We can use our phones to deposit checks. Realistically, I rarely visit the bank because virtually everything is handled online. I pay all my bills online, and it works out well that way.

For my business checking account, however, I am required to go to the bank to deposit those checks. They do not have an online phone application for business checking as they do for personal checking. So here's the *but* (you knew it was coming): About a year ago I started to notice a pattern. Every time I went to the bank to make a deposit, they would try to up-sell me something—a new credit card, a new loan, or some other financial service. In most cases, I simply wasn't interested because I have enough credit cards, I don't need a loan, and I don't really need (or want) any of the services they were offering.

I understood that they were just trying to do their job, but to be honest, it became a little frustrating. This went on for several months. One day I said to one of the tellers, "Can I ask you a question? Every time I come in here, you guys are trying to give me a new credit card or something like that. What's the deal?"

They said, "There is new management in the home office, and they want the tellers to make the customers aware of all the services the bank offers."

They were required to sell or promote new credit cards, home loans, car loans, etc., to reach sales quotas every week. The teller went on to tell me if they did not meet their goal, they were viewed as not being very productive and could potentially lose their jobs.

I told the teller, "Look, I appreciate what you're trying to do, and I understand it's your job. But to be honest with you, it's becoming annoying. I use your bank because you're convenient. I like what you do here. I've been satisfied with your service, but every time I come to the bank, I get frustrated because I feel like I'm going to get pressured into applying for something else I don't really want or need. I get the fact that the home office is requiring you to do this, but at this point I'm ready to move to another bank because I don't want to be sold anything else. If I need another credit card or loan, I promise you I will talk to you about it."

I was nice about it, and she understood. I asked her if she would pass my message on to the management. "You're pushing away customers. You are not helping make sales. Your management needs to be on the front lines so they see firsthand how it affects customers. I respect that your company goals are to make more money; that's why we're all in business, but this is not the best way to go about it."

I was pleased that not long after all the branches stopped pushing products. The tellers simply went back to their standard banking processes of receiving checks and passing out money. Apparently, the bosses in the home office got the message.

Up-selling is a normal course of some businesses, but in this case, the tellers were driving away long-time customers. I think one of the important takeaways in this story is the disconnect between the corporate offices and what really happens on the front lines of the business.

Corporate leaders make choices that on paper seem logical, and when they do the math, they get giddy over the potential for new profits. However, if they don't understand their customers and the experience they want, they are putting their employees in difficult situations and may even drive business away. The message is simple: Before you make sweeping changes, go to the front lines, talk to your staff, and find ways to accomplish your desired outcome without driving a wedge between you and your customers.

The battle for business survival in the future must be tied to customer satisfaction first with a long-term goal of customer loyalty. Any salesperson worth their salt will tell you it's easier to keep a customer than to attract a new one. That was true forty years ago, and it's still true today. The big difference is that everything you do, say, price, sell, fix, or distribute will be publicized somewhere on the Internet, and *you* are no longer in control of the message.

This may sound like a never-ending battle with few prospects for success. Nothing is further from the truth. Because if you offer good service, produce a valuable product, price it fairly, guarantee results, and support a culture that strives for customer loyalty, the positive reviews and online chatter will propel your business forward.

Reflections by Carol:

During my career, I worked for a large real estate brand which had both company-owned and franchise affiliations throughout the country. I personally had experience on the company side, leading a large franchisee organization, working for the franchisor, and ultimately the parent corporation that owned multiple franchise brands in multiple industries. I realized I was a rare breed in the organization because I had sat in every seat and had seen the business from every perspective.

What it taught me was that every element of a business has its own agenda and its own goals. It's not enough to say that each is focused on profit. Over almost three decades, our company was independently operated, owned privately by holding companies, owned by a major corporation, and ultimately publicly owned.

Without going into long and boring details, some information is worth sharing because it points to the complexity and necessity of all elements of working together for an outcome that serves every level of the organization.

Let's start with the customer. In a real estate organization, there are two customers: internal and external. The external customer is John Q. Public, those people who entrust the sale or purchase of their home to the company and the sales associate they hire to represent them. This is the person who pays the commission at the end of a completed transaction, and the revenue earned fuels everything else in the corporate food chain. It compensates the sales associate, pays toward the costs of the local office, and contributes to the franchise fees on the affiliate side or to the revenue to the regional company-owned offices. From there a portion of the revenue goes to support the corporate offices and ultimately the investors or shareholders. Needless to say, there are a lot of mouths to feed and a lot of rent to be paid along the way.

The second customer in a real estate organization is the internal customer, but they have different names and definitions depending on the level of the organization. Real estate is supported first and foremost by the sales associate, those men and women on the street in every town and city who are customer-facing. In real estate, the majority of sales associates are independent contractors (ICs), not employees. According to the IRS, that means they are self-employed—an employer (the real estate broker) cannot control the time they work or the services they perform.

The expectations and compensation agreed to between a real estate broker and a real estate sales associate are detailed in an Independent Contractor Agreement. Because the ICs can move their license to another brokerage firm at will, there is a great deal of incentive for forging relationships that meet their financial and business needs. These are your most important internal customer.

In all companies, employees are internal customers and should be managed accordingly. This includes things like compensation, benefits, training, work environment, culture, etc. Employees are critical to running any business smoothly, and turnover is costly and disruptive.

In a franchise organization, there is another critical internal customer: the owner of the real estate business who signs a franchise agreement to do business under your brand. In exchange for the use of the brand identity and advertising or marketing support, the franchisee or affiliate agrees to return a portion of their revenue to the franchisor over the term of the agreement in the form of royalty or franchise fees. Depending on the industry and the franchisee, other operational guidance, services, awards, events, training, and systems are made available to the network so that franchisees can grow and flourish.

But there is the potential for breakdown at every level. If sales associates feel that they are not getting the support, the leads, or the commissions worthy of their talents, they are free to leave and can do so at any time. If their production represents a significant portion of that office's revenue, this can leave a gaping hole to fill.

Employee retention is one of the most worrisome issues for all businesses today, not just real estate. It takes time and money to attract the right talent, and it can take up to two years for them to reach optimum productivity and mastery of their job. Companies are furiously trying to come up with solutions to engage, promote, develop, challenge, and compensate workers so they stay longer and contribute longer-term value to the organization.

The relationship between the franchisee and the franchisor is often the most vulnerable, for a very simple reason. The franchisee is in the business of selling real estate (in my example), or changing oil, cleaning houses, cutting hair, selling sandwiches, running a fitness studio, painting houses—the list is endless. The franchisor is in the business of selling franchises and collecting royalties. If the two are at odds, the results can be costly. The franchisee may struggle because they are not receiving enough support to be successful. If the franchisee is failing, then no royalties are being paid and the income required to grow the franchise is limited. It is a true catch-22.

Regardless of the simplicity or complexity of your business, it is critical to understand how all the pieces fit together. The consequences of decision, choices, and policies should be carefully thought out, taking into consideration their impact at every level and on everyone concerned.

I had a long and blessed career, and I am grateful for all the opportunities I was afforded. But in the end, my career goals pulled me back to my entrepreneurial roots. I grew up in a family-owned restaurant. There wasn't a role I didn't fill both in front of the house and the back of the house. It was the best training one could hope for in terms of customer service, food handling, pricing, business operations, and marketing.

But rather than tell my story of entrepreneurial risk and adventure, I would like to share Bonnie's story.

Have you ever heard a commercial for a new product and thought, *That was my idea years ago! Why didn't I invent it?* If you have, you were making a choice to *not* take action. We've all done it in some form or another. Bonnie Tyler's story starts out that way. Over the years, she had many good ideas of products people couldn't live without, things that would make our lives better. But like most of us, she put her ideas aside, and sooner or later someone else got the idea to market first . . . until one day when everything changed.

Bonnie had been asked to bring deviled eggs to a party. She was running late, and at the time she should have been arriving at the event, she was standing over her sink trying to peel a dozen eggs. The eggs were not cooperating. Pieces of shells stuck to the whites and shredded the smooth outer surface.

"I knew there had to be a better way to do this. My ugly eggs made it to the party, but I vowed to find the gadget that would make peeling hard-boiled eggs easy. There had to be something out there. There was a gadget for everything else!"

It turned out that the only product for peeling eggs performed worse than doing them by hand, and it took up way too much space in the kitchen. Bonnie made her first critical choice that day. She would not rest until she developed a solution for peeling hard-boiled eggs.

It is important to point out that she had no knowledge or experience in manufacturing, product, packaging, or distribution. She was co-owner of Cyber Sidewalks, a web and graphic design company in Fairfield County, Connecticut. Her business partner, Sheila, was the graphic designer and knew CAD (Computer-Aided Design).

They took the idea in Bonnie's head and began designing it using CAD software, and then they created a prototype using a 3-D printer. Bonnie said the 3-D printer made all the difference in being able to test their idea without the cost of manufacturing. It took six months of trial and error and over seven iterations before they had a product in hand that worked. All this was done at the Westport Library with the help of Dimitri, an eleven-year-old whiz kid who was working on his own design for a prosthetic hand.

"I remember the 'eureka moment' when I placed an egg in the prototype with a little water, shook it a few times, and the shell fell away." Bonnie knew she was really onto something. At this point many inventors will rush around to friends and family and show off their new idea.

First piece of advice and choice number two: Go to a lawyer and file for a patent. The drawings from the prototype were registered, and Bonnie and Sheila were on their way. The key to their design and what makes it different than just shaking an egg in a glass jar is the bumps. Little nodules circle the inside to create enough friction to crack and separate the shell from the egg. This was the true birth of the Negg™.

Once the patent was secured, they began demonstrating the Negg™ to anyone and everyone. Friends raved, family asked to be the first to receive the product, but the real test was the enthusiastic endorsements they received from professional chefs. This thing worked, people wanted it, and now they had to figure out how to get it from prototype to consumer product.

The path to success, as usual, was anything but smooth. Bonnie made a commitment that the Negg™ would be manufactured in the United States, and ideally she wanted to work with a company in the Northeast so she could be close to the process. Together, she and Sheila talked to tons of manufacturers. Most were skeptical and said it couldn't be done. The way injection molds are designed could not work with this product because there would be no way to extract the mold if they insisted on the internal bumps. Finally they found a manufacturer willing to work with them on the design and ultimately came up with a solution for a collapsible mold.

The stumbling block was the cost. The mold alone would over $64,000, and that didn't include one single Negg™ being produced. Discouraged but not scared away from their goal, they decided they needed to raise capital. They launched a Kickstarter campaign, hoping to raise enough money to cover the cost of the mold. The first campaign fell short of their goal and left Bonnie and Sheila with a decision to make. *Do we give up, or do we forge ahead and keep trying?*

What happened next represents the most important choice in this story. When you truly believe in something, you know it can work, you know it beats the competition, and you know it can make money, you have *no choice* but to go forward.

Bonnie shared with me that it was their own naivety that kept them on course—that, along with the determination to succeed. They stood up to engineers who wanted to change the design. They stuck to their commitment to U.S. manufacturing when others were advising them to take it overseas. They crushed every naysayer along the way, learned from their mistakes, and forged ahead.

The second crowdfunding campaign was successful, and they raised most of the money needed to start the manufacturing process. But now another choice had to be made. "Do I reach into my savings and take that final step?" Perhaps the choice to do just that and sign that manufacturing contract was the most difficult choice of all, but by making that decision, the first Neggs™ were in their hands ready for Christmas delivery on December 2, 2016.

At the beginning, they did all the fulfillment from their office in Connecticut. They had over 2,500 orders to fill from the 970 backers during their Kickstarter campaign. But how many more could they sell? Where should they sell? How would they continue to market the Negg™?

Today they have outsourced the fulfillment to a company only thirty miles from them, and Neggs™ are flying off the shelves. You can find them on their website, NeggMaker.com, as well as on Amazon and The Grommet, and their debut on Home Shopping Network sold out in fourteen minutes!

"The challenges aren't over," Bonnie says. "When you make consumer products, you are always facing issues with manufacturing deadlines, packaging, labeling, shipping, wholesale orders, and customer service. Every day is a new beginning."

By Bonnie's own admission, "The point of no return was when I pulled the trigger on the mold. I did go into my savings to cover the difference between what the crowdfunding campaign raised and what we needed to cover costs. It was full steam ahead because there was no choice. It was just a feeling in my gut this was going to work."

Her advice to anyone who has an idea (for anything) is to believe in yourself and your ability to make it happen. "Don't let the voice in your head talk you out of it. Don't listen to people who don't know what they're talking about. Absolutely don't be afraid to ask for help. So many amazing people along the way seemed to appear just when we needed them most and guided us to the next step."

The choices made in this story are easy to identify and be inspired by. What may not be so obvious are the values that drove Bonnie forward. Without a doubt she is creative and determined. After all, she came up with this idea while she was standing over a sink peeling eggs. She went forward with zero knowledge or experience in manufacturing, patent law, packaging, shipping, fulfillment, sales and marketing, raising capital, or crowdfunding, but nothing held her back.

"I know now that it also took courage and my ability to take risks to get us where we are. Those values that held me back with other ideas, but they propelled me forward on this one."

Courage and risk-taking are essential values for anyone who wants to succeed in business. It may not be a product you imagine you could bring to market. Maybe it's a choice to open a new location, introduce a new service offering, invest capital during an economic downturn, or surrender responsibility. Courage and risk-taking are values that can easily be weakened by a balance sheet or the cautions of others.

True success comes to those leaders who are willing to take a chance even when the outcome is questionable. After the research, the due diligence, and the financial analysis, the final decision always comes from the gut. Do you truly believe this is the right path?

Bonnie and Sheila have transformed their business focus and their lives, and it's all because of the Naked Egg—oh yes, that's what Negg™ stands for. Hopefully you will never have to peel an egg again, and when you use yours, you'll think of Bonnie and what it took to get that little gadget in your hand.

20 | CHOICES

Wow, so how does a corporation or small business owner handle all the different aspects of their business? How do they make choices and decisions that satisfy everyone?

It's a conundrum because differing goals affect the choices made, and they are often in conflict with each other. The stockholders want to see a return on their investment, which may mean raising prices and reducing overhead. The customer wants great products or service at a reasonable price (a.k.a., the Walmart effect). The owner or manager wants employee retention and bottom-line profit so they can remain in business and provide for their own families.

Look at the airline business. Over the past few years, airline travel has become painful at best. A few years ago, you could purchase a ticket, use your miles for an upgrade, get a meal or a snack, plus check your bag all for one price. Easy peasy. Not anymore. Now there are so many layers and options, it makes your head spin. Do you want First Class, Business Class, Economy Class, or Cattle Class? Do you want to board first, have an aisle seat, a window seat, or a seat with more legroom? That will cost you $75. Oh, and you want to check a bag? No problem. For an additional $25 per bag, the airline succeeds in accommodating you and ticking you off at the same time. And good luck trying to book with those hard-earned miles today. With some airlines, you now need 100,000 miles just to fly across country in coach.

This whole process could be streamlined and made easier by using some common sense and implementing a one-pay fee. But, as it has been said for years, the death of common sense has drastically affected this country. The airlines seem to make choices based on the value of the bottom line, not on providing a superior customer experience. Customer service gets the seat in the last row of the plane next to the restroom.

The question you must ask yourself is this: "Is my company focused on the customer or solely on the bottom line?" Believe it or not, it is possible to make a great profit and have happy and loyal customers at the same time.

But sometimes the greed and self-interest isn't coming from the corner office or the board room. Sometimes it comes from the very people you depend on to run your company. What do you do when a member of your staff is holding you hostage?

Reflections by Carol:

I made a choice some years ago to fire my top producer. I was managing a large real estate office made up of eighty-four sales associates. In most real estate offices, there is an imbalance between those who produce heavily and those who do very little production. Our office was no different. We had a very strong office and a very productive office, but our top producer still represented a significant portion of the revenue.

Iris had been with the company for a long time—over twelve years. And with that tenure and production, she had grown to enjoy a list of privileges from the company. Shortly after I took over the office, we moved to a newer, larger facility, and one of the things she had negotiated was a private office. This was not usual in our company, but not uncommon in the marketplace.

The other agents had either semiprivate offices, a cubicle of their own, or shared cubicles if they were new to the business or part-time. Iris was thrilled to be getting her own private space. She had brought her husband and daughter into the business to assist her, and both were given individual cubicle workstations just outside of her office.

We moved into our new facility in July, and the office flourished. As the end of the year approached, Iris's husband asked if he could take me to lunch to discuss their contract for the coming year. I was curious why he was making the request instead of her, but I agreed. When we went to lunch, he presented me with a letter outlining the things they expected the company to do in the coming year for them to stay and not take their licenses to a competitor.

The first item on the list was that the company would agree to do an additional renovation (at company expense) to block off more space so that the husband and their daughter could be part of a private office suite. In preparation for our meeting, he had reached out to the contractor who did our renovation, who estimated the work would cost approximately $35,000.

Number two was they wanted the company to pay for and install a private phone line that would go directly to Iris and bypass the front desk receptionist. It's important to note here that this was before mobile phones and VoIP. The offices operated on a landline and central voicemail system. At the time incoming calls to the office were handled by a "duty agent," and buying and selling leads were theirs to pursue. Eligible full-time agents were put on a rotating calendar, dividing up the times the office was open. If callers specifically requested an agent by name, they were redirected to that agent.

The third request was that Iris's "team" would have a monthly allocation for them to spend on advertising at their discretion. The amount requested was nearly the same amount of money we were spending on the entire monthly office advertising budget.

The fourth request had to do with relocation referrals. We were a relocation company, and the leads that came into our office were assigned to experienced associates who had gone to relocation training to be certified. Of the eighty-four agents in the office, there were fifteen who were certified to receive relocation leads, including Iris. Iris and her husband wanted a guarantee that their closed-deal income from any relocation business would be $50,000 by the end of the year. There is no guarantee that any relocation lead will result in a closed sale, so the number of leads needed to achieve their stated income requirement could not be calculated in advance.

The last request was that the company would increase Iris's commission to 95 percent and guarantee that percentage for as long as she stayed with the company. At the time, she was being paid at 82 percent, which represented the top level of the company commission schedule. In real estate, the commission from a sale is paid to the real estate broker who, in turn, pays the sales associate based on an independent contractor agreement and prescribed commission schedule tied to production. Our company's commission schedule ranged from 50 percent for new associates to 82 percent, depending on prior year earnings. The company paid for all office expenses, salaries, advertising, and rent, leaving the associates only responsible for their own personal marketing and expenses related to their real estate license and association dues.

These were the choices that Iris's husband laid out for me. I said to him, "I appreciate you taking the time to share this with me. I know you are aware that this is obviously out of the norm of what we offer to our sales associates. I do not have the authority to make this decision on my own, but I will consult with senior management and get back to you. For me to properly represent Iris, and assuming we can't do everything, can you prioritize for me what the most important items on this list are?"

He answered without hesitation, "These *are* our priorities. There were other things we wanted, but we already took them off the list. These are the things we need to stay."

I said, "OK, I understand. I'll get back to you." It was a very civil lunch. I didn't react, nor did I disclose any opinion on any of the requests. I did ask a few more questions just for clarification about what they had in mind for the office renovation. I also asked him how we would measure the relocation business.

I had already made up my mind that the price was too high, but I felt I needed to consult with senior management. Iris had been with the company for over twelve years, and I had only been with them a little over a year. I also knew the culture of the company was to make exceptions for a top producer; this was a common practice in the industry. Real estate is a relationship business. I knew and respected the value she brought to the office. She was very skilled. She was well liked, both within the office and within the real estate community. Iris was known as a tough but reasonable negotiator. My sense was that this list of demands wasn't coming solely from her but was being driven by her husband.

I met with senior management, sharing first the letter outlining the list of demands. They had a strong and immediate reaction. They asked me, "Is there anything on this list that would appease her? We obviously can't and won't do everything—it's ridiculous."

I shared the answer that Iris's husband gave me when I asked the similar question. I also went on to explain that my belief was that they weren't bluffing, and they were not prepared to negotiate. We knew Iris was being aggressively recruited by a competitor who offered higher commissions but didn't cover any expenses for his associates. In fact, there was a monthly fee assessed to each associate to cover office expenses outside of commissions.

Senior management asked me what I recommended. I said, "I don't have an office of one. I manage an office of eighty-four sales associates. And while Iris represents significant gross revenue, after allocation of expenses based on space and usage of resources, the net profit from her production is negligible. If we agree to any of these requests, our return on investment from her production would result in a significant loss. In addition, it would have a profound negative impact on the other sales associates."

I went on to explain that I felt my responsibility was not just to this individual but to the other eighty-three agents. For those reasons, I recommended that we agree to nothing. We would be opening ourselves up to demands from other agents in the higher-production quadrant. We would also run the risk of losing other agents who were contributing to the profitability of the office, and we would lose incoming leads and potential relocation business.

I set up a meeting to take place at 4:00 p.m. on Monday in our office conference room with Iris, her husband, and her daughter. The timing of the meeting was strategic because weekly office meetings took place on Tuesday at 9:00 a.m. Regardless of the outcome of our Monday meeting, I would need to address the office the following morning.

When the three of them arrived, they were startled to realize the meeting was only with me, that senior management was not in attendance. "Thank you for meeting with me and allowing me time to review your requests with senior management. Iris, my understanding is that this is a non-negotiable list and if we cannot agree to everything you have asked for, your intention is to terminate your relationship and move your license. Is that correct?"

She paused, looked at her husband, and then turned to me and said, "Yes, this is what we need to stay."

I responded, "Then this is going to be a very short meeting. We cannot and will not agree to anything on your list, and your association with this company is over today. We respect everything you have done and wish you only the best wherever you choose to go. I have boxes ready for you, and I need you to have your office and workstations cleaned out by 6:00 p.m. I'll collect your keys before you go."

I stood and waited. Iris burst into tears and ran from the conference room, slamming the door. Her husband and daughter raged at me until I raised my hand and quietly said, "These were your demands, and you left us no choice." I moved to the door and walked back to my office.

It was 6:45 p.m. before they were completely moved out; the tears had stopped, and the calls to friends had run their course. I locked the office and went home, sad but secure that I had made the right choice.

At 3:00 a.m. my phone rang. It was the local police informing me that the front door had been shattered and the alarm was blaring. It only took me fifteen minutes to get to dressed and reach the office. When I arrived, I saw that one full panel of our double-glass entry door was gone. We used my key to open the remaining door, and on the floor in the lobby we saw a large brick.

The police did an inspection, and I verified that nothing appeared to be stolen. Their conclusion was that vandals must have thrown the brick. I knew better, but I saw no value in pressing charges. There were no security cameras in those days, and I had no proof. We called someone to clean up the glass and patch the door with plywood until it could be replaced.

When the agents arrived the next morning for the sales meeting, the first thing that greeted them was a plywood door. Some already knew about Iris; others didn't. All were understandably upset and confused.

I called the meeting to order and began, "I am sorry to announce that effective immediately, Iris is no longer associated with our office or our company." I allowed time for the gasps from the unknowing and tears from her friends. "It's important for you to know that this was my decision, and you deserve to know why."

I read the letter in its entirety, watching their faces as the reality sank in. "I want to tell you why there was no alternative—and it's not really about why, but who. I am responsible and accountable to eighty-four associates in this office, not just one. I could not support special exceptions and excessive demands that would have hurt you. I love and respect Iris, and I truly wish only the best for her. After today I will not talk about or discuss this further, but I will answer any questions to the best of my ability."

One of the agents asked, "Are we going to be OK? She was our top producer."

I answered, "Yes, she was, and her production will be missed. However, we are strong and profitable without her contribution."

Another agent stood, one of Iris's closest friends in the office. "We have work to do. If every one of us just does one more sale this year, it will more than make up for Iris. Are you with me?"

The entire office stood and clapped, and someone shouted out, "We're behind you!"

To say that this was one of the most difficult choices of my life is a gross understatement. I was faced with immediate loss of production, potential loss of other associates who would follow (none did), a tarnished reputation for me and for our office in the real estate community, and other potential fallout.

The easier course may have been to give in and agree to the demands while trying to figure out a way to make it up to the other sales associates. I can honestly say that, at the time, I didn't make the decision based on values at a conscious level. I also didn't make the decision to let Iris and her team go because I wanted to win. I did the math and knew economically it would have been disastrous for the office and the company.

When things finally settled down and I had time to reflect, I realized that the values buried deep within me were what guided me through that episode. It was through the feedback I got from my sales associates, my peers, my superiors, and others in the real estate community that I began to understand how values played such a vital role.

In my head, I had always thought that I made good business decisions, but decisions with heart. I could look at the numbers, plan for the future, and implement based on goals and objectives. It all sounds very clinical and proper—right out of the MBA manual. And there's nothing wrong with that.

But underneath the spreadsheet is another piece of paper that every manager and every leader has. It is the *Values that Guide Me* manual we have been given and helped write during our lifetime. The challenge we face is how often we check in to see if we are being true to our values. Have they changed? Do they own a different priority in our lives?

In the situation with Iris, the values I tapped into were community, fairness, loyalty, responsibility, and self-respect. And if I were truly honest with myself, I would have to add courage. I wasn't thinking about those values at the time. I was making the choice based on instinct and evaluation of cost and impact. But perhaps that's enough.

Running a business is tough. Markets are volatile. Taxes can be backbreaking. Good employees are hard to find and harder to retain. Customers are fickle. So why do so many of us choose to be entrepreneurs? What motivates us to want to run our own businesses?

Because while the risks are high, the potential rewards are even higher. When you make a choice to go into business, you are in charge of your destiny. The battle for position, raises, benefits, and time off evaporates. You are making the decisions. No one can fire you but you. And oh yes, you will never work harder in your life. It's been said that entrepreneurs will work eighty hours a week to avoid working forty. It's not for everyone.

There is equal pride and satisfaction in working for someone else. Perhaps your choice is to be part of a larger team working for a company that gives you the income and personal satisfaction you desire. No matter how large or small a business is, it can only succeed through the efforts of its people.

The more you understand what values drive you, the easier it will be for you to carve your path in the business world. After all, we spend between forty-five and fifty years of our adult lives working to make a living and save for retirement. How you do that is up to you. Is the choice you made the right one? This leads right into the next chapter on Career and Work.

CAREER AND WORK

*Stop chasing the money and
start chasing the passion.*
TONY HSIEH

WHEN YOU THINK about the number of hours, weeks, months, and years that we spend working, it is no surprise that our lives get out of balance. Whether you are a representative in a call center, an executive in a large corporation, or a stay-at-home mom raising the kids, each job requires endless hours of commitment and dedication to fulfill those roles.

Was your career a choice or was it accidental? Are you in a job to pay the bills while you are preparing for your dream job? Have you been in the same job for a long time and are you still happy with that choice? What would you like to change?

During the recession that started at the end of 2007 and ended midyear in 2009, thousands of people had their worlds turned upside down due to job elimination, consolidation, or company closure. The concept of job security evaporated, and workers at all levels and in all industries began to look at their work and career through a different lens. Even for those who remained employed, raises were frozen, benefits were slashed, and pensions were eliminated.

Adults were suddenly faced with the prospect of having to redefine their very purpose and role in the workplace because the job they had yesterday no longer existed. The silver lining in this chaos was that it provided a wake-up call for us to look differently at work and career. Starting over was not just an option; it was the only option, and no matter your age, education, or experience, life was offering new choices.

How you spend your waking hours is one aspect of your life that you have complete control over—*if* you choose to manage it. If what you are doing is nothing more than a job to pay the bills, then chances are you are not satisfied and haven't found your ideal work or career.

Reflections by Alan:

Recently Penny and I had the opportunity to see the band Chicago perform in Dayton, Ohio. Chicago has been together since 1967; if you do the math, that's fifty years. Over their career, they have sold over 40 million units in the U.S., with twenty-three gold, eighteen platinum, and eight multiplatinum albums. They've had five number one albums and twenty-one top-ten singles. They were inducted into the Rock and Roll Hall of Fame in 2016. Chicago is one of the most recognized bands in the world. Four of the original founding band members are still with the group, and they are all roughly seventy years old!

When my wife and I went to this concert, we had the opportunity to meet the band before the show. I asked the group, "How have you managed to stay together for so long? How do you choose how to operate the band, and how do you choose what music you record and play?"

James Pankow, the trombonist of the group, said, "We just have so much fun doing what we're doing that we don't really worry about anything too much. We just go out there and have fun."

I would have to agree with him after seeing them in concert. They definitely have fun! We had excellent seats in the third row, very close to the stage. We could actually see these gentlemen play their music. It amazed me to watch these guys, who are all past retirement age, play music and having an absolute blast just doing what they're doing. If we could all find that kind of passion in our work, the world would be a much better place and a lot happier.

Obviously, these guys are talented, and they've worked hard to be where they are. Incidentally, both James Pankow and Robert Lamm were inducted into the Songwriter's Hall of Fame in 2017. Congratulations, gentlemen!

They have the talent, they put in the time and the effort, and in turn, they have a blast and continue to be passionate about what they do. They made a choice to be in the band. They made a choice to stick with the band long-term. In doing so, they also made a choice to be away from their families, be on the road touring, and spend countless hours in recording studios. For many in the entertainment industry, this is too big price to pay, and that's why we see so many burn out way before their time.

One of the things I've heard from other entertainers and speakers who are in the public eye is they absolutely love what they do when they are onstage. Whether they are musicians playing for a crowd or speakers delivering a keynote message, they love being in front of an audience. That's their natural high. That's what they live for.

And yet the other thing they have in common is that they hate the travel, being on the road and away from their families. But again, it is a choice.

They are willing to spend 90 percent of their time doing the things they hate in exchange for that one hour on stage. It all comes down to commitment, passion, and choice.

One of the things I have discovered is that the people who find their passion, figure out the one thing they are good at and love to do, and put all their energy into pursuing it are the most successful.

Too many of us just dabble in things. We will play around with this a little while and then lose interest. Then we move onto something else and play with that for a little while, and then we decide we don't really like that either. You do have to spend some time trying to find what it is you are truly passionate about, but unfortunately too many people spend their entire lives dabbling and never quite latch on to that *one* thing.

In the classic movie *City Slickers*, Jack Palance's character, Curly, asks Mitch, played by Billy Crystal, "Do you know what the secret of life is?" [He holds up one finger.] "This."

Mitch: "Your finger?"

Curly: "One thing. Just one thing. You stick to that, and the rest don't mean shit."

Mitch: "But what is the 'one thing'?"

Curly: "That's what *you* have to find out."

We all face that challenge, and knowing when to tune in and tune out to the messages others are sending can be frustrating, confusing, and lead you in the wrong direction. We are all given a handful of talents; we just need to figure out what they are and how to use them.

In the case of the band Chicago, they found their talents, and in doing so they have entertained the whole world with their music. James Pankow said, "We've been together for fifty years, and I hope we'll be together for fifty more." Now that's a legacy!

It may be easy to dismiss the magic of what keeps a band like Chicago together for over fifty years. After all, doesn't everyone fantasize about being a rock star? A glamorous life on the road, thousands upon thousands of raving fans, and of course the money keeps rolling in.

For most of us, that dream never becomes a reality. We are stuck in our mundane lives doing what we need to do to get by. This next story is about someone who loved his job and his corporate career but was adversely impacted by the recession. His journey and what he learned about himself may provide some hints for you on your own perception about work and career.

Reflections by Carol:

There are some people you meet in life who are destined to become part of your universe. For me, one of those people is Ken Herron. We worked together at Realogy from May 2006 until November 2007, when the downsizing occurred. Ken was our vice president of Interactive Strategies, and he brought a fresh new perspective to the company and its brands for leveraging the Internet and led our companies to become the industry leader in innovation and Web 2.0 marketing.

He has the innate ability to think outside the box and explore new tools and techniques that companies rarely pay attention to because they are too deep in the weeds running their *businesses as usual* using tried-and-true methods from the past. We were no exception.

Ken came to us with years of corporate marketing experience, having lived through the transitions from AT&T to Lucent to Avaya. He was used to bureaucracy and endless meetings, but his boundless energy and enthusiasm propelled us into new cutting-edge marketing.

After Ken's position was eliminated due to the looming recession, he was scooped up by several other companies over the next few years. He always made his mark in a short period of time, but being last in, he was first out on three successive occasions through no fault of his own.

During this time, we stayed in close contact. I had launched my own business after leaving the company in 2007 and leaned on him to be my guide for online marketing. When you are a fledgling business with a very small budget, your options are limited, or at least they used to be before social media. My success and the very reason I became America's LinkedIn Lady has been because of Ken. He encouraged me to try new things and test the boundaries of this new media for my business.

But this story is not about me. It's about Ken and what he has done and continues to do to keep his career moving forward and his future prospects bright. Ken uses Twitter more than any other social media platform and has grown his network to well over 135,000 followers. He engages with people all over the world and leverages those relationships to his advantage.

Ken plays a critical role for Unified Inbox Pte. Ltd., a Singapore-based intelligent IoT messaging company on the brink of explosion in the IoT and AI space. Where that goes remains to be seen, but an important note here is that, regardless of where it goes, Ken has equipped himself with a new set of skills that will serve him well. He continues to invest to stay on the cutting-edge of technology-driven marketing.

This background should give you a picture of his work ethic, his open-mindedness, and his can-do attitude. Nothing stops him and nothing slows him down. He is the most disciplined and goal-oriented person I know. So, what's his message?

"I was gainfully and consistently employed for so many years that when the job gaps happened during the recession, I wasn't fully prepared. I did the only thing I knew how to do. I treated looking for a job like a *job*."

Ken created a routine and a system for searching, posting, and following up on possible positions that would make any project manager proud. Every day he committed a minimum of four hours to job search (more if opportunities presented themselves).

"While I saw friends or former colleagues wallowing in self-pity and fear, I stuck to the task at hand. I needed to find not just my next job but my next environment where I could flourish. And until I did, I wasn't going to stop." Once Ken landed a new position, he dove in headfirst, giving it his usual 110 percent.

He shared that when there are forces outside your control and you find things to be the opposite of what is normal for you, you must avoid all negativity. During that time, many people fell into the Groundhog Day trap of reliving their past career over and over in their head, trying to recreate or resurrect something that no longer existed.

When you are in a situation that is the opposite of your normal, there's a lot less sanity and a whole lot of doubt that can creep in. If you reach into your own toolkit and lay out in front of you what your unique background, skills, and experience bring to the party, you're able to go from insecurity to confidence and you get a clear picture of how best to market yourself.

The other thing that Ken did that is worth pointing out is that when he wasn't spending time job searching, he was investing time to learn and grow. He kept himself current on everything that was happening in this bullet-train environment. "The beautiful thing about the Internet is that all the information you need is there; you don't need a big corporate budget or even a staff to stay current. You only need to apply yourself."

Before he committed full-time to his next company, he had a robust consulting practice supporting individuals, companies, and organizations to execute a social media strategy that he helped them to create.

I asked him how he compares the corporate life with the life of an entrepreneur. He said, "There is something to be said for being a big fish in a smaller pond. I need to be able to make a difference, and I can do that every day. On top of that I have the potential for reward unparalleled with the raises and bonuses I got when I worked for corporate America.

"I feel I'm doing work that matters and is appreciated. When I worked for AT&T, I had to wear my white shirt every day, sit in a salary grade-appropriate cubicle and beg, literally beg, for every computer I ever had. Now if I need a new device, I just buy it. No procurement, no endless business-case justification, and no politics."

In Ken's world, the tools change daily, and with the ability to try new things with no IT department to block downloads, he has the freedom to explore and evaluate. There is no "that's not how we do it here."

We all have experienced our new devices becoming obsolete within eighteen, six, or even three months. As entrepreneurs, we have agility, independence, and the autonomy to make decisions, but only if we seize it. Ken says, "Companies are never going to be at the forefront if others are judging or second-guessing their decisions."

Today Ken uses his mobile phone as a resource for everything. He vets potential clients; researches new tools; takes, finds, enhances, and posts images and videos to social media; and communicates with people all over the world using text, Skype, Viber, WhatsApp, and sometimes even a good old-fashioned phone call.

"There was a bit of an OCD (obsessive compulsive disorder) culture at AT&T; it's true for most big corporations. I learned the rules and knew what could and couldn't be done. Now I make my own rules, and I can change them in real-time as the needs of my customers, partners, and business require."

I asked Ken why he has chosen now to work with Unified Inbox. I knew he had many other opportunities to work with other leading tech companies. "That's easy. It's the people. They're at the right time in the right space, and there is huge potential for success."

Something else that Ken pointed out was that this has validated his schooling. He studied International Economics with a second major in German as an undergraduate and received his master's degree in International Management (MIM) in Marketing. Like most of us, he didn't know when, where, or even how those degrees would benefit him, but today it is crystal clear. Unified Inbox is truly a global company, and the members of the team represent a different kind of diversity. As he travels the world on business, he has encountered people who practice fifteen hours of fasting, zero tolerance for drugs or alcohol, and crimes that are punishable by death that would be misdemeanors in this country.

"I continue to learn from our global customers. I work daily with people in Singapore, China, India, the United Arab Emirates, and Germany. Technology is now the sacred "T" of business, and in the case of Singapore, they have taken *green* to a new level. They put the US to shame."

Despite what may seem like a glowing, almost fantasy-like picture of a life and career, Ken is the first to admit it hasn't come easy and has only progressed because of hard work. His key lessons for all of us are actually quite simple:

- Whatever you do, it's always your choice and it always has been.
- You are who you are—stop trying to change it—just do what it is that you do best.
- Evaluate your strengths and focus on the ones where you can give yourself a "ten."
- Nobody else can figure it out for you.

When I asked him if he would ever return to corporate life, he said, "I'm incredibly fortunate. I no longer have to work in an environment where what I do best is not valued. It would be very hard for me now to work in a slower-paced environment where I had no control."

He went on to say, "You can only make the leap when you're ready. It's just like losing weight or joining a gym; no matter how painful or how urgent it is, you won't act until you're ready."

The most interesting thing Ken shared in this interview was what he attributed his success to and what advice he would give to others. Surprisingly it had nothing to do with his degrees. It came down to this:

- *Take a typing class.* "It was the most useful skill I ever learned, and I use it every day."

- *Get good at public speaking.* "I was absolutely not comfortable doing it, and because of that I wasn't very good at it, but it is an essential skill that now serves me every time I face a client or an audience."
- *Become a writer.* "When you learn how to capture and communicate your ideas, you are in complete control."
- *Learn a foreign language.* "Other countries still do this better than the US. Studying other languages didn't just teach me my own, but has enabled me to access the world."

Ken ended by saying, "We live and die on our skills. Everyone has innate strengths, skills, and talents, but too many people ignore them or don't keep them current."

Making choices—whether they are easy ones or hard ones—is something we cannot avoid. One of the biggest takeaways from Ken's story is that, regardless of what you do, who you work for, how large or small your company is, only you can make the right choices for each stage of your career. Do not depend on others to do it *for* you, or you may end up with others doing it *to* you!

Maybe you are a nurse, an engineer, a business owner, a dentist, a doctor, a lawyer, a plumber, or a traffic cop. Are you doing what you're doing because that is what you wanted to do or because someone else pushed you into it?

For generations, careers were often carved out of the family stone. Doctors beget doctors; lawyers birth more lawyers; tradesmen take over the family business; and generations within families proudly wear the blue uniform. There is nothing wrong with this as long as the person taking the baton truly wants to run that race. Do not wake up twenty or thirty years down the road realizing you never wanted to follow in someone else's footsteps. Your occupation is among the most important choices you will ever make.

We have both seen Jack Canfield do this exercise with his audience. He pairs people up and one person asks the other, "What do you want?" After they answer, you ask again, "What do you want?" When they respond, you ask again, "What do you want?" This pattern can go on for twenty to thirty minutes, but there is a point. By forcing someone to dig deeper and deeper and deeper, you reach the heart and soul of what they truly want—and it's rarely the first, second, or even third answer.

It's a good lesson as to why choices can be difficult. Much of the time we are making our decisions based on a superficial level and not on the meaningful, deep-seated level.

When it comes to choosing a career path or profession, it is not enough to get an education or pursue a path because the job market has openings in that area, or because the family legacy dictates it. Don't choose a job because it sounds easy, or it pays well, or it doesn't require a degree. Those are diversions that lead you away from choosing the right direction for yourself.

The choice of what you do with the rest of your life must include passion. The acid test is being able to look yourself in the mirror and ask, "Is this what I want to do for the rest of my life? Does it give me pleasure? Do I look forward to the next day? Should I be doing something else?"

Ponder this story. There was a dentist who became a dentist because his father was a dentist. He knew it wasn't what he wanted to do, but his father pushed until he got his way. The son hated being a dentist from the first day. He had no passion for it whatsoever, and this lack of passion reflected in his work. One day, quite accidentally, he hurt someone performing a dental procedure and was sued. It cost him hundreds of thousands of dollars in legal fees and a damaged reputation. Finally, when someone pressed him with the question "What do you want?" over and over again, he blurted out, "I don't want to be a dentist anymore." It was the first time the words had ever escaped his lips. He gave voice to the feelings he had been suppressing for years.

Our good friend Dan Miller of 48 Days has numerous stories of people who are absolutely miserable in their jobs. When pressed as to why they don't find something else, they usually answer with weak responses. They only have five years to retirement. This is the only work they know. They make a lot of money, but the work stirs no passion. Please understand, we are not suggesting leaving a job simply because you don't like it. We have both worked several jobs over the course of our lifetimes because of family responsibilities and such. You must take care of responsibilities. However, that doesn't mean you must stay there for your entire career. In days' past, a tradesman might work in the same line of work for forty-plus years. Today, most college graduates will have at least a dozen different jobs/career changes in their working lifetime. Career choices made by an eighteen-year-old are not necessarily the same choices made by a forty-year-old. Remember, you are not a tree. You can pick up and move.

When was the last time you really thought about what you are doing with your life? Is it what you want to be doing for the next five, ten, twenty years, or more? Are there choices you could make today that would propel you in a different direction? What will you do to explore those options? What will you have to give up short-term in order to achieve that long-term benefit? What skills do you possess? What passions lie within you that could transform your career? Maybe the first choice is to take that first step.

EDUCATION

*Education is what remains after
one has forgotten what
one has learned in school.*
ALBERT EINSTEIN

THE TIME HAS passed when a high school education is enough to prepare you for the future. Today, a college education is expected. High school seniors are expected to achieve at least a bachelor's degree before they enter the workforce. If their chosen profession dictates, some will go on for a master's degree. The good part is that young people are more educated today—but are they any wiser? Is the pressure to pursue higher education worth the effort, time, and money that they put into it? While not popular, these are questions every one of us should think about and ponder—whether you're a parent or a young person.

At seventeen or eighteen, it is difficult to decide what you really want to do with your life. If you have thought about this and have an occupation in mind you wish to pursue, the necessary type of education you will need is easier to determine. But what if the direction that interests you doesn't match the needs of the market? Should you pick your major based on the potential for future earnings? Chances are parents and guidance counselors will say yes.

The most recent studies on this subject make it crystal clear that anything in the fields of engineering (electrical, mechanical, biochemical, aeronautical, industrial, software, systems, even nuclear and mining) or in computer science dominate the charts. Only two jobs in health care rank in the top thirty according to PayScale's 2016–2017 College Salary Report. This includes physician assistants and dental hygienists.

We can't look at the top paying jobs out of college without looking at the worst paying jobs. These include art, theater, health services administration, biblical studies, English teacher education, broadcast communication, paralegal, special education, early childhood and elementary education, culinary arts and food service management, human services, social work, youth and pastoral ministry, and child development. Clearly there is a pattern away from soft skills to science and math. But there is also a concern about the future for doctors and lawyers and teachers.

Reflections by Carol:

When I went to college, it was with the dream of changing the world. I wanted to make a difference. American University in Washington, D.C., offered political science and psychology—two subjects that fascinated me. Truthfully, I wasn't thinking about how I would make a living. I guess I considered being a psychologist, but I had no idea what I would do with a degree in political science. It didn't matter. I just liked the subject.

It did afford me the opportunity to work on Capitol Hill for my congressman throughout school. The influence of that experience convinced me to claim poli-sci as my major. Great until I left school with an education that equipped me to do . . . well, nothing!

I returned home for a year to help my parents sell their business and retire to Florida, but my heart was in Washington, D.C. They encouraged me to go to law school. I had the grades and aptitude, but I didn't have the interest. I had no idea how I was going to make a living, but I knew I would figure it out. Luckily I picked up some fundamental clerical skills along the way, so I secured a job as a legal secretary. Perhaps a few years hanging around lawyers would motivate me toward law school. It didn't.

At the end of my first year, I knew I didn't want to punch a typewriter (research that on Google if you don't know what it is) for the rest of my life, and I *definitely* did not want to become a lawyer. Next I went to the classified ads in the *Washington Post*. My goal was to find something that interested me, paid more, and wouldn't require an advanced degree.

I saw an ad for a real estate salesperson: accepting applications, no experience necessary, will train. It was perfect. I could keep my job during the day and work evenings and weekends until I got established, and I only had to take one course and one test to get my license.

In February while I was doing my taxes, I took the time to compare my earnings. I had worked a full year in the law firm, and my W-9 reflected $7,500 in earnings. I had worked six months in real estate, and my 1099 reported commissions of $8,000. Now, I'm no rocket scientist, but even I figured out I could make more money full time in real estate. I quit my day job and never looked back.

What started out as an accidental second job became my career. Over the next few decades, I owned my own brokerage company; managed a large firm, where I headed up training locally, regionally, and nationally from the corporate headquarters in California. I was part of the expansion growth team for the company seeking to enlarge their footprint in the Northeast. I headed operations for our largest affiliate company in Hawaii, and ultimately I ended my corporate career as the senior vice president of operations.

For the past ten years, I have been living my ultimate dream as an entrepreneur, pursuing my passions and tapping into the skills and experience I amassed along the way. None of this makes me smarter or more talented or luckier than anyone else. I just committed to hard work and continuing self-education, and I trusted in the fact that new opportunities would open when I was ready. Not bad for someone who graduated with a non-marketable degree in political science!

All of us are given certain talents. Some of us have more than others. When we think of talents, we often think of someone who can play a musical instrument or sing, or an artist who can paint or draw. But talents go way beyond the arts. Maybe your talent is interacting with people—you can calm anyone down, you are an active listener, and you help people solve personal problems. Maybe you're one of those people who can fix anything around the house. Or maybe your talent is inspiring young minds. Regardless of what the most lucrative jobs and the recommended degrees suggest, if you are on an educational path that doesn't support your talents, you are going to have an uphill climb.

Try asking yourself, "What am I good at?" and then ask your friends and family, "What do you think I'm good at?" The answers may be similar, but you also may be surprised by their responses. People who know us well often see things in us we don't see in ourselves. Conversations like this can open new possibilities for what your life's work should be and will help you decide what kind of education you need to move forward.

We sometimes live too close to ourselves to recognize our own potential. We can't see the forest for the trees. And even if you are aware, you can easily devalue your own talents and abilities. "Sure, I can play the guitar, but that's just something I do," or "Yeah, I like to do that. It's no big deal. Nobody really pays attention to it." It might be a very valuable talent that could help other people or provide a career path that you hadn't considered.

Once you choose your direction, then pursuing the right education to get you to your goal becomes easier. The options are many: undergraduate college, graduate school, community college, trade school, online degree or certificate program, or apprenticeships.

Reflections by Alan:

When I was in school, we had a shop class where we learned how to use tools and do woodworking. We built birdhouses and lamps and tables and learned to work with our hands. At home, Dad always had my brother Steve and I helping him fix things around the place. I used to think I spent my entire teenage years behind a Gravely tractor working in the garden. I didn't understand, appreciate, or even enjoy it at the time, but I am really glad my mom and dad made me do chores around the house. Dad taught me to become familiar with tools and not be afraid to fix something that wasn't working. I find it amazing today that many people, especially men, don't even know how to hold a screwdriver, much less use one. To me, that is sad. What we are going to find as time passes is that we have many educated people, but no one knows how to fix anything.

Presently, I work in a college environment, and I see this every day. Unfortunately, I feel our education system is lacking in several areas. They teach history. They teach economics. They teach sociology, psychology, and higher math. But they leave out many important real-life skills, such as how to balance your checkbook, how to invest money in the stock market, and how to maintain your car. Schools have eliminated home economics and shop classes. Most people do not even know how to sew a button on a coat anymore. They just buy a new coat! We can recite the dates of the Livonian War, but we can't solve an everyday life problem. Please understand, I believe a college education is a wonderful thing; everyone in my family has a degree. Nevertheless, many very important life skills are not learned in a classroom.

It seems everything has moved toward the intellectual side of the fence and away from the labor side. Everyone can't be a desk jockey. Everyone can't be the boss. For example, there's a lot of money to be made understanding computers, networks, and programming. Today, there are degreed programs for computer science, but many jobs don't necessarily require a college education. And there are other very lucrative occupations that don't require a degree at all but provide a good living and lifestyle; electricians, plumbers, mechanics, builders come to mind. These jobs may not be as glamorous as sitting in the corner office of a downtown high-rise building, but they may play to your strengths, and after all, money is money and we all must pay the bills. Why not pay the bills with money you earn doing something you love?

Tapping into your talent is a good first step, but matching that with your passion is when the magic happens. It is prudent to set realistic goals. Just because you were the quarterback of your high school football team doesn't mean you'll be drafted by the NFL. Just because you play a mean riff on your guitar doesn't mean you're going to be the next Jimi Hendrix. It's no secret that only 1 or 2 percent ever make it to the "big time" in any profession.

Those who do make it have a few things in common: They seek the education they need, they practice and work hard, they master their craft, and they probably have a little bit of luck along the way. It has been said it takes ten thousand hours of consistent practice and work to master any craft or talent. In real terms, that is working forty hours a week for five years at that one thing. Most folks don't want to put in that kind of time.

If we're discouraging you, that's not our intention. The goal is to aim high but also build in a back-up plan. The best college athletes get their degrees. The most talented musicians know that tastes change, audiences are fickle and you can be a hit today and a bum tomorrow. They always have a backup plan. What is your Plan B? How about even having Plan C and D? If something you are aspiring to doesn't work out, what is your backup plan?

This reinforces why some form of education is essential for you to succeed in life. But after you finish trade school or college, does the learning end? Absolutely not! Education is a lifelong journey. Don't be that person who hasn't read a book since high school. Take advantage of the many free webinars, online courses, podcasts, and training programs available. And the biggest secret of all is to open yourself to learning new things outside of your chosen field. Don't be the person who is so one-dimensional that when your job vanishes because of economic shifts or changes in demand, you are left standing alone with no alternative.

We recommend you seek out information on subjects like how to start a business, how to run a business, how to speak, how to write, even how to listen. Even if you stay on the same path for your entire life, this added knowledge will make you better at whatever you are doing. And if your commute to work is longer than ten minutes, over time, you can get the equivalent of PhD knowledge on any subject just by listening to audios in your car.

Hans Hanson is a nationally recognized college advisor with a passion to help families during the college recruiting and admissions process. It was his own experience with his son, a Division 1 baseball player, that put him on this path to guide parents and students in making the right decisions and taking advantage of the resources available to them.

Hans' message to students and athletes is: "You have to be in the game, involved, engaged, and adjust where needed. Graduate on time with a meaningful degree." But he also advises that there isn't always a straight path to what you want to do; there are different ways to achieve the same outcomes.

His own path to success took many turns, and his college experience spanned twenty-two years. When he started, in his family there were three siblings in college and a nine-year old at home. He knew his dad was struggling, and he felt guilty because he wasn't living up to his potential.

"I wasn't ready for college. I knew I needed to grow up and regain credibility and respect within my family and for myself. I knew I was going to disappoint them if I continued the path I was on. The choice I made was to drop out of school and join the Air Force."

His whole life changed with that one decision. "I was helping out the family by reducing the expenses of college; I instantly got paid; and the Air Force was going to pay for my education. I needed discipline and structure, and that's what I got."

Hans spent five years in the Air Force, two of those in Colorado and three in Germany, where he mainly did accounting and finance. "I'm proud to say I received the Air Force commendation medal for outstanding performance at both bases where I served."

That experience opened the door for him to return to college and receive his degree in accounting (not political science, which had been his original major).

He got married and had two children of his own. After a few years in accounting, he pressed on to get his CPA—passing the exam in one sitting. His determination to do the very best wherever he was became a beacon from the lighthouse for his life.

In 1985 he changed careers, location, and direction to join the family business, a printing supply company providing packaging supplies for paper mills. This was the second major transition point in his life. His dad was chairman of the board and wanted a family member in the business. He had two other partners, but he wanted to assert more control over the business, possibly to take it over in the future. Hans had turned him down three times, but facing a high cost of living where he lived and the responsibility of young children, he realized moving back to his hometown would be a better place to raise his family. He thought, "If it doesn't work out, I can always return to being a CPA." He worked there for fourteen years until the business was sold in 1999.

"I realized during that time that my goals were to become my own man and be accepted by my parents. I also knew I wanted to spend the rest of my life teaching kids how to take control of their lives.

"Most people let life happen to them, and they hope it turns out good. In my work with families and kids going to college, I see them going through the process blindly and hoping it turns out OK. My mission is to move them from hoping to designing and planning."

Rarely does someone have such clarity around the single choice they made in life that became that pivotal moment that put them on the path to success. For Hans, it was his independent decision to drop out of college and join the Air Force. Having the courage to make that choice when parents, siblings, counselors, and even society were pulling him in a different direction could not have been easy. "I took a big risk to change," he told me, "but it was my life-changing moment."

When you wake up and realize life is not going the way you want it to, what choice do you make?

Hans' advice is to look inward. What are your capabilities? What do you want others to think about you? Making a choice for yourself builds the confidence to keep moving forward and take other risks.

"We aren't born successful, but when we work hard and make well-thought-out decisions, things will happen. Only one out of ten kids are making their own decisions instead of what their parents want." Parent should have input, but when young adults have the final say in how their future is going to play out, they are more committed to the outcome.

The right decision is rarely the easy decision. Hans believes there is no room for regrets. If things don't go the way you planned, learn from them and move forward. "I'm a perfect example of that. I could have dwelt on the fact that I didn't do well in college at an early age, in my freshman and sophomore years. Instead, I made a choice to change my situation, in spite of the fact that I knew I would hurt and disappoint others. But it was the right choice for me.

"Society is besieged with the notion that there is only one way to do everything. Success comes from being decisive and taking action. I believe you should evaluate, reassess, develop, and keep moving forward."

When we discussed values, it was no surprise to me that his core value is self-esteem. "For me, I think the prize in life is always about a feeling. With everything I do, I want to feel good about myself and my family. When I joined the Air Force, it wasn't to *be* in the Air Force or to fight for our country. I joined because it was about feeling good about myself . . . about acceptance."

The way to assess any life experience is not to ask, "How did you like it?" but rather "How did it make you feel?" The earlier you identify and latch on to your value system, the better choices you will make.

In truth, our values were created by our families, going back generations. Even if they aren't discussed, our behaviors teach values. You don't have to reinvent them. The sad truth is that if you don't have a value system to guide you, you are going to make some very bad decisions.

The Internet has made it impossible for parents to control exposure and information. We are challenged more today than ever to raise kids with values because of the easy access to counterculture information and disinformation.

Create the image you want for yourself—you are branding yourself all along the way.

Jim Rohn left behind pearls of wisdom to be passed on to new generations. One that applies here is: "Formal education will make you a living. Self-education will make you a fortune." Certainly, we would love everyone to walk onstage and get that diploma, but whether you do or not, make the choice to be a lifelong learner.

Charlie "Tremendous" Jones says it a different way. "You will be the same person in five years as you are today except for the people you meet and the books you read."

And here's a final tip. Education is a critical key to future success, but so are the people with whom you associate. Jim Rohn said it best: "You're the average of the five people you spend the most time with." The reason behind this is simple: You have similar interests, go to similar places, and live in similar surroundings. You may also share similar educational backgrounds and job experience. In other words, you are in your comfort zone when you are with them.

If you are not satisfied with where you are in life, look around at those friends. Are they challenging you to be better? Are they aspirational in their own lives? Are they making more than you or less than you? Do they discourage you from taking risks? It sounds harsh to imply you may need to find new friends, but that might be the truth.

If you are the most successful person in your group of five, then begin to associate with people who make more money than you, who own their own successful businesses, who are doing the types of things you would like to be doing. It will open a whole new world of possibilities. By raising the bar of friendship, you automatically raise yourself up.

In the end, the best education is everyday life. Seize each moment with enthusiasm; listen, observe, digest, and inhale. Never stop learning!

ENVIRONMENT

*The ones who are crazy enough
to think they can change the world,
are the ones who do.*
Anonymous

THIS IS ONE of the shorter chapters in the book, but it may be the most important.

We all live on this one planet. Technology has exploded over the past hundred years, from horse and buggy to the automobile to the airplane to the Jet Age to the Space Age. It's hard to believe that it has been almost fifty years since a man landed on the moon. In that period of time, we have vastly increased our knowledge of science and technology, environment and nature, yet there's still a whole lot we don't know. Hardly a day goes by that you see or hear news about global warming or climate change. The question is: Is this real? What should we do about it? What choices can we and should we make in our everyday lives that can positively affect this planet?

Perhaps you have been following the news about sending a man to Mars. Space is fascinating; what kid doesn't want to be an astronaut? Space is sexy; it's the new frontier. Given the political climate and the resources allocated to support NASA programs, it is unlikely that a Mars landing will occur in our lifetime. When and if it is accomplished, it will likely be from the private sector. But when will that happen? It could take decades. There is just too much technology that has yet to be developed before we can put a man on Mars—and an even longer time before we could send a significant number of people to colonize a planet that far away.

That means we need to take care of the planet we have. While the news reports a steady stream of updates on our planet's health, opinions are deeply divided on how bad it is, how quickly it is changing, or even how soon life as we know it will come to an end. Those ringing the alarm bells are at war with those who read the data differently. And even when the scientists agree, the politicians do not, and special interest groups only serve to deepen the divide.

In a recent conversation with Chuck Peavey, the executive director for the Business Environmental Coalition, we asked him about global warming. We also asked him to recommend some of the things we can do and the choices we can make to help improve this planet. He confirmed that most of the research is politically motivated. Politicians have changed the terminology from *global warming* to *climate change*. Global warming sounds too ominous; climate change sounds more manageable. Well, of course, the climate is going to change. He referenced reports that say 97 percent of the environmental scientists agree that people are affecting the climate. However, he cautioned that those numbers are misleading. There are about fifty thousand environmental scientists in the world. A survey was sent out to roughly ten thousand of these scientists, and about 3,200 responded. Of those responses, only seventy-nine were fully qualified to answer the questions that were posed. Seventy-seven of those scientists said that humans are *probably* a contributing factor; 3 percent said, "No, not that much."

News outlets say the ice caps are melting, but data shows that Antarctica has more ice than ever. To confound the views even more is the fact that we only have about one hundred years of reliable temperature data on the planet. Yet, depending on your viewpoint, religious or scientific, the planet is either six thousand years old or it is millions of years old. Realistically, one hundred years out of millions of years (or six thousand) is barely a blip on the radar screen. Do we really know what we are talking about at this point? Yes and no. What we can agree on is that air, water, and land pollution are contaminating our earth, and the effects on human life cannot be ignored. Just talk to someone from Flint, Michigan, affected by lead poisoning in the water, or Niagara Falls, New York, after the discovery that 21,000 tons of toxic waste had been dumped into the abandoned Love Canal. Perhaps you remember the Exxon Valdez oil spill in Prince William Sound, Alaska, and its impact on the habitat for salmon, sea otters, seals, and seabirds. These are just a few example—and only in the United States.

Regulation and government oversight can set standards and help to avoid future disasters. But what can *we* do as individuals? One of the best things we can do is to pay closer attention to the trash we create. Every plastic bottle, every Styrofoam container, and every non-biodegradable object we dispose of contributes to this ever-growing crisis.

A very real concern right now is plastic in the oceans along with all the other trash that is ending up there. This is a planetwide concern. There are gyres (vortexes) in each ocean filled with thousands of tons of plastic that have washed into them, either due to flooding or people just throwing stuff in the water. Charles Moore discovered the first gyre in 1997 on a sailing trip through the Pacific. The issue is that plastic never really breaks down, but over time, becomes fine particles. The turtles, the fish, and the aquatic life eat the plastic, thinking that it's food, but it is not digestible and usually ends up killing them. Scientists are concerned that if this trend continues, we're going to ruin the oceans—not by overfishing, but by polluting our oceans with plastic.

Of course, this creates a controversy. Some environmentalists believe it best to leave the plastic in the ocean today and let it work itself out on its own. The task is enormous, and the expense to clean the oceans cannot even be calculated. Their solution is more regulation to prevent more plastic from ending up in the ocean in the future. Plastic by its nature has a static charge. It affects and attracts toxins electrostatically, which just creates a more vicious cycle in the food chain. These toxins get into the fish and are passed on to humans when they are caught. And what exactly are those fish sticks in your freezer actually breaded with? Hmmm . . .

So, what should we do? According to Chuck, regulations won't solve the problem. Politicians are more likely to enact new laws regulating abuse than allocate resources to attack the problem head-on. Companies have teams of lawyers dedicated to finding ways around the regulations, so how effective are they really? The private sector has the greatest chance of uncovering new solutions and ultimately profiting from their research in how to handle trash.

Small businesspeople are problem solvers. While government promises to provide more jobs, small businesses create the bulk of the jobs in this country. Knowing that businesses, whether large or small, have the problem-solving skills and varying resource capabilities to tackle these environmental issues, why then aren't we making more progress? Perhaps the answer to that questions lies in getting the public sector and the private sector to first agree on critical issues to be tackled, and then enact legislation that stimulates growth and allocate resources to help businesses move forward.

Since that conundrum is not going to be solved anytime soon, we as individuals must take the proverbial bull by the horns and act. Getting people to act starts with awareness. Let's go back to our plastic and its effect on the environment. How many units of bottled water do you consume in a day?

One? Two? Five? Each one of those, if not properly recycled, will end up in a landfill and too often, in the ocean.

But plastic bottles are only the tip of the iceberg. Consider your use of polystyrene (aka Styrofoam). While there has been some progress is limiting its use and production (some cities have even banned its use), the problem is far from solved. Styrofoam is non-biodegradable and non-recyclable. According to research done by Washington University, it takes five hundred years for Styrofoam to decompose. In addition, it releases large amounts of ozone into the atmosphere, causing both respiratory and environmental issues. It is estimated that Styrofoam products take up over 30 percent of our landfill space.

Do you own a Keurig machine? If you do, you know how convenient it is to make a cup of coffee in less than a minute and everyone in the house or office can pick their favorite. There's no more scorched coffeepots and no more drinking sludge. However, have you considered the impact of all those K-cups going to the landfill? John Sylvan has, and he's the man who invented the Keurig coffee pods. "I wish I'd never done it. The pods cannot be recycled as a whole."

It should be pretty obvious by now what we should be doing. Start by limiting—or better yet, eliminating—the use of all non-recyclable plastic and polystyrene products. We must each make a choice to minimize as much trash as we can. Don't throw everything away. Some items can be repurposed, reinvented, or reused. If your municipality provides recycling, then recycle. Local authorities recycle in different ways. Some have separate bins for glass and plastic and paper. Others may provide only one bin. Believe it or not, the one bin system requires that workers go through the trash by hand to separate materials. If your town has taken the position, "It's not worth the trouble. Just throw it away," then apply pressure for change or seek private companies who recycle for profit.

If you want more information on this subject, just go to Google. Try searching words like *non-biodegradable, zero waste companies, polystyrene*, and *plastic recycling*. There is a wealth of information to help you fully understand why this is so important and how you can help save the planet. It's a simple choice really. If each of us does our part, the combined effect may not stop the problem, but it will certainly stem the tide.

The values underlying this choice are lofty but worth embracing. We don't necessarily think about citizenship, idealism, or the desire to leave the world a better place as values we focus on every day. But when you put your toes in the sand the next time you go to the beach, do you want to see plastic and debris floating in with that tide?

FAMILY AND FRIENDS

*Walking with a friend in the dark is better
than walking alone in the light.*
HELEN KELLER

WHAT IS FAMILY? According to Dictionary.com, a *family* is "a basic social unit consisting of parents and their children, considered as a group, whether dwelling together or not." To be fair, they have added a definition for a *single-parent family* as "a social unit consisting of one or more adults together with the children they care for." *Merriam-Webster* defines *family* as "a group of individuals living under one roof and usually under one head." Both references seem a bit stilted and somewhat dated. Our favorite definition comes from UrbanDictionary.com:

> A group of people, usually of the same blood (but do not have to be), who genuinely love, trust, care about, and look out for each other. Not to be mistaken with relatives sharing the same household who hate each other. REAL family is a bondage that cannot be broken by any means.

Wow! Now we're getting somewhere. While there are still examples of the "Ozzie and Harriet" traditional family of the fifties, our world has changed, and there are fewer "traditional" family units (Mom, Dad, and 2.3 children) and more variations of social units living together as a family.

However, one thing has not changed. Family is about loving and supporting the people you share your life with. Whether you are the parent or the child, the husband or wife, the grandparent or the in-law, or the person who joined the tribe from outside the bloodlines, you are family.

When you are part of a family, every choice you make affects the others.

If Dad gets a job and transfers to another state, it impacts school, friends, church—all things familiar. If Mom makes a choice to go back to her career after the kids are in school full time, who will make dinner and do the laundry? If your older brother decides to join the Navy, who will play ball with you and teach you to talk to girls? If your sister gets into drugs and gets arrested, what are the repercussions for everyone else? And if Mom and Dad decide to get a divorce, what happens to the children, the rest of the family, or even the dog?

It's easy to see how potentially fragile the family unit can be, and yet through time, nothing is stronger or has lasted longer than family. No friendship, no government, and no authority has the same power over our lives as our families.

This brings with it an enormous responsibility and commitment. It's not all about you; it's about your relationship with those special people in your life. It truly gives the word *choice* a deeper and more significant meaning. Where do you divide the line between choices that are in your best interest and choices that are more favorable to the family?

There is no easy or single answer to that question. For instance, let's say you are living in a dysfunctional family where Cheerios and vodka serve as dinner most nights, the phone rings incessantly from bill collectors, and the police show up on a regular basis because the neighbors reported hearing screams. What choice do you make? Do you stay and try to fix things? Or do you walk away and put as much distance between you and your family as you can?

This is the perfect time to introduce Cheryl's story. Her situation as a young teen will break your heart, and the journey to find her way to freedom was long and arduous. Years later, she wrote these words:

Happy Mother's Day
A Special Thank You from Your Daughter

Thank you for teaching me these important life lessons:
No matter what comes my way—I am a SURVIVOR.
Always look at the glass as half full.
Cooking, cleaning, and taking care of a household shows you care.
Sickness can be conquered by a positive attitude.

Never go to bed with a grudge—always forgive.
Live each day as if it were the last.
Music and nature heal all pain; drugs and alcohol just mask the pain.
Do not trust all doctors.
Unconditional love is the best gift you can give a child besides being by their side during difficult and happy times.
Never compete with your children.
Never forget a birthday of a loved one—it is a special day to celebrate.
Actions speak louder than words—saying the words "I love you" means nothing when you do not back it up.
Giving of yourself not only helps others but makes you feel good.
Your looks will come and go, but who you are as a person is what truly matters.
When one door closes, another door opens.
Words can have long lasting impact—choose them wisely.
Most importantly—I AM ENOUGH.
Your daughter,
Cheryl

Her story tells the rest. "I had become my mother's mother. When she drank too much, fell asleep, or crashed the car, I was always the one there to pick up the pieces." Cheryl spent her childhood in fear and despair. No matter what she did—cleaned the house, prepared the food, worked to get good grades in school—it was never enough. "I could never understand why I was so unlovable. The harder I worked to please her, the nastier she became."

Growing up, the pattern of Cheryl's life played like a worn-out record. Birthdays were always forgotten. She would wait at the curb to be picked up by the car that never came. She dressed in unflattering clothes that camouflaged her voluptuous body so as not to compete with her mother. She was always compared to her brothers and her sister and grew up feeling like she was a disappointment and a failure.

Imagine a childhood plagued with self-loathing and unending embarrassment brought on by the actions of your mother. Where Cheryl found her joy and her voice was in school. She got good grades and found solace in music and the arts. Her teachers loved and appreciated her. She was naturally talented, but beyond that, her passion for music was pure, and it was the only thing in life that allowed her to escape and give her joy.

The night that changed everything happened when a steely-eyed police officer approached her. "Are you OK?" he asked. "What are you doing hiding in this bush at three o'clock in the morning?"

Cheryl told him, "My mother broke all the windows in the house and told me she would kill herself if I did not leave immediately."

He replied, "Where do you live?" She told him. "You will have to come in and file a report. Do you have anyone you can stay with tonight?"

Cheryl was sixteen years old, and that night a shift happened that put everything into motion. She went to stay with a friend, but she still had to deal with the school, the investigation, and her mother. When they sat together in the school office with the counselor and her high school music teacher, it did not go well. Her mother made her out to be the evil child. She shrieked at them, "You don't know her!" Cheryl recalled that the pure hatred she saw in her mother's wintry green eyes numbed her heart.

For the next seven years, Cheryl was on her own but not fully detached from her mother. She would travel from where she was living by train to visit occasionally, but it never ended well. When Cheryl was twenty-three, the situation changed. Her mom had lost her license after crashing her car while driving drunk for the third time. She came to live with Cheryl on weekends so she could work as a nurse's assistant after losing her job at Emerson Hospital. Then she would return home by train during the normal workweek.

Cheryl would receive calls from her in the middle of the night threatening suicide. Cheryl had heard this song her whole life, and finally she had had enough. She made her choice. She changed her number and refused any further contact with her mother.

You could argue the choice was tough love, but it was so much more than that. The choice was freedom. To escape her past and to carve a new path, Cheryl married and became an Orthodox Jew. She thought that changing her name would change her life. Cheryl immersed herself in the strict tenants of the faith. She was devoted to her husband and their two children.

But things were not as they seemed. Her children were growing up with resentment and challenged the limitations imposed on them in this household. The devotion she showered on them and her husband was not being reciprocated, and she felt alone. When she realized that things weren't perfect, she also came face-to-face with her own unhappiness. She had built a wall around herself and her family, but she recognized that she was living a lie. The choice she had made to seek freedom and distance from her mother was, at best, a Band-Aid to protect the wounds of her youth. She wasn't really healed, and she knew she couldn't be until she found herself.

She divorced her husband and moved out to finish raising her son, who was in eighth grade, and daughter, who was in high school. But even that was tumultuous. Her husband lived close by and played the indulgent parent, offering the children a safe haven when Mom was too strict. During all the rebellion and tears, she did the only thing she knew to do—offer them unconditional love no matter what.

As this new chapter began to unfold, she received the call telling her that her mother had had a stroke. Cheryl was forty years old, and it was time to cross that bridge. Her daughter was fifteen years old and had never met her grandmother.

Things between Cheryl and her mother never really changed, but Cheryl saw her in a new light. She realized that her mother had a disease. Seeing her mother with this new clarity, she could finally accept the fact that her mother loved alcohol and drugs more than she loved Cheryl. "I couldn't get mad. I couldn't cry. I could only feel sorry for all that we both had missed. In the following years, we spoke occasionally, but we never fully reconciled. When she died, I felt nothing."

Cheryl shared that what got her through every phase of her life, every crisis, every hurt, and every joy, was that she always had a surrogate mother. She sought and received love from others who saw in her what her own family tried so hard to crush.

"Above all, I always felt most accepted when I was in tune with nature—the sacredness, the quiet serenity, and the music that filled my heart." She had given herself the greatest gift of all: the gift of survival.

Her deepest unflinching value is her own spirituality. Her journey to living the life she was meant to live came from deep within her soul. When she sings, performs, writes, or meditates, it is that oneness with self that shines through.

One of her favorite quotes is from Anne Frank: "I keep my ideals, because despite everything I still believe that people are really good at heart." That belief allowed her to find a new love—someone who appreciates her, supports her, and encourages her to be herself.

I asked Cheryl why she kept her maiden name when she married her new husband. She smiled and said, "Because it took me a long time to find myself, and I'm not going to give up my identity."

We talked about the lessons she learned along the way and what she would like to share. Here's what she said:

- Don't wait for things to happen. Take charge and make things happen.
- Quit being so hard on yourself, and stop saying "I'll never be enough."
- You can't control how people treat you, but you can control how you react.
- Don't let the little things wreck your life. Connect with your inner child and be joyful.
- You can't run away and hide from your family, and you can't use religion as a shield.
- Set out to make a difference. You will make mistakes, but you will grow. That's what life is all about.
- Above all, embrace your imperfections and love yourself.

Cheryl advises anyone in a dysfunctional family to realize you have no control if you remain in that situation. Your control is on the outside. If you wallow in self-pity, nothing will change, and it only leads to more bad things.

Cheryl's values stretch way beyond spirituality. It is also clear that the values she learned and embraced came from outside her family. Throughout her life, it is the search for love and acceptance that anchored her belief in love. Everything she does and everyone she touches experiences her kindness, optimism, honesty, and inner harmony. The value that shines the brightest and surrounds Cheryl like a halo is courage.

There are times when family will triumph over tragedy. Throughout our lives, we are faced with choices where we could go either way. There are positive and negative consequences, and there is no clear right answer. But we must decide, even if we're not sure. This is when your commitment to family values counts the most and your personal needs or ambitions have to be weighed against the greater good of the family.

Reflections by Alan:

In 2004 I was working for a cable company. I was doing well and was reasonably content with my job. However, I had previously worked in the automotive industry, and to be truthful, I missed that kind of work. It was a very satisfying type of work for me. An opportunity came about after one of my previous co-workers had moved to South Carolina. He called me one day and said, "Hey, I would like to hire you to come down and work on my assembly line."

I said, "OK, let's talk." I had been to this plant before so I was familiar with the area, familiar with the plant, and familiar with what they produced. I knew quite a few people who worked at this facility, so if I did take the job there, it would be a very easy transition. My college roommate also lived in the area along with several other acquaintances. And my wife and I liked Spartanburg and the Greenville area of South Carolina.

We agreed on an interview time, and my wife and I drove down. I went through the interview and took the twenty-five-cent tour of the plant. They told me what I would be doing and offered me a position with decent pay, moving expenses, and so on—a very nice package. Needless to say, I was very interested in this opportunity.

On the drive home, Penny and I pretty much made up our minds that we were going to do this. We wanted to move. We were ready for a change. We started to discuss *how* we would do this. We'd have to sell the house, move all our stuff, and find a place to live in Spartanburg. But nothing discouraged us. We were really excited about the new job and the prospect of moving.

What worried us most was telling our parents because people from our area rarely leave the state. There are deep family ties, and you are expected to stay close to home. We planned how we would tell them and assure them that we weren't moving that far away and would be back often to visit.

At the time, our boys were ten and fourteen years old. What we were not prepared for was their reaction. When we announced that we were thinking about moving to South Carolina, they had a meltdown. One started and the other chimed in.

"We can't move."

"All of our friends are here."

"We grew up in this house. We have all of these memories and we can't move."

"We have to stay here. This is our home."

Penny and I were shocked and surprised at how affected our boys were with the possibility of moving. They absolutely did not want to move. It caught us both off guard, and we were not sure what to do. To be truthful, it really bothered me. I remember thinking, *I really want this new job . . . but can I do this to my boys?*

Previously my wife and I had agreed that kids are portable. You can pick them up and move them with you; they will adjust, and they will love South Carolina.

I asked the company to give me a little bit of time to think it through while I pondered what would be the right choice for me, Penny, and both Justin and Jesse. In the end, I decided to turn down their offer. It was a hard decision because I really wanted to go to South Carolina and I really wanted the job, but I felt (and Penny agreed) that the boys' happiness was more important than us *possibly* having a better job with *maybe* more money. I chose to put our boys first.

I later discovered that several of the people I had worked with from the stamping plant in West Virginia had accepted the job offers and had moved to Spartanburg. Truthfully I kind of felt left out. Surprisingly, though, after about a year or so, most of them came back to West Virginia. They all said it just wasn't what they thought it would be.

In retrospect, I realized I had dodged a bullet. I didn't disrupt my family, didn't have to go through the house selling and buying process, and our lives remained intact. Today I still live in the same house, my boys are now grown up, they are through college, and everyone is happy. I have a great job, a great family, and a great life.

I made the choice to look out for my boys, and in the end it benefited all of us. While going through the interview process, I was certain I was meant to move, but thankfully, when put to the test, I listened to the whisper that said, "Look after your boys first."

Is blood really thicker than water, or does the modern interpretation of family transcend bloodlines? That's up to you. In our view, family is what you make it. In addition to the family you were born into to, there is the family that you create for yourself. But when you do become part of a family, remember that while your choices become more complicated, the rewards are so much greater.

This next story is about family, friends, and how sometimes we have to force breakups in order to find our way. Those choices are never easy.

"I left the motel and got in her car. I vowed I was not going back. I got on the freeway with the intention of having a fatal accident. I didn't want to die, but there was no escape, no options, nowhere to turn. I couldn't find anything to crash into; eventually I ended up back at the motel. I figured maybe this would send the message home. 'You're an asshole, Mom.'"

Christopher Rausch was sixteen years old and had been homeless since he was thirteen. Their gypsy life included motels, garages, vans, and the backseat of a car. He had to steal to survive. And, despite their circumstances, his mother managed to keep eighteen cats and four dogs in her care. Christopher dropped out of school in the seventh grade and fell off the radar screen.

Even before stealing her car, he had tried to take his life. He swallowed half a bottle of Advil. He just wanted someone to care about him. He was surrounded by drinking, smoking pot, and nameless men who came and went.

Maybe next time I'll just kill myself, he thought to himself. That wish almost came true in the weeks following. A man threatened him with a gun when he wouldn't buy a carton of cigarettes. "He thought I wasn't buying because I was white and he was black, but it was because they weren't menthol—that's the only kind I smoked."

Christopher faced the man and the gun, saying, "Go ahead and kill me!" He had hit rock bottom, and had his friend not stepped in to save him, he would not be alive to share his story.

In his misery, he knew he had three options: die, go to jail, or leave. It was his choice. Something deep inside of him wasn't going to allow the first two options to prevail. He also realized that until he stood up for himself, his mom wouldn't take care of herself—a very sage insight for a young man. He kept telling himself, "I'm the most important person in the world and I'm the only one who can change my situation." The question was *how*.

Jobs were in short supply for a dropout with no permanent address, but he was hired on as a telemarketer. The pay wasn't enough for him to leave, so he got a second job at Carl's Jr. But he couldn't strike out completely on his own yet. As fate would have it, the owner of the telemarketing company was closing shop and moving to Texas. He told Christopher and his friend (who also worked there) that they could take over his apartment. Together they cobbled sufficient earnings to move into that apartment, and life looked like it was going to change.

He went back to the motel to tell his mother he was leaving, expecting her to be supportive. Instead she wailed, "Who's going to take care of me?" And that was the nicest thing she said to him. She called him every name in the book and raged until she had no more energy to continue.

Christopher remembers saying, "I'm leaving the motel, but I'm not leaving you. I have to go out and live my own life. I'll still support you, help with the cats, and such. But I'm doing it."

In sharing this recollection, he laughed and said, "I decided I wasn't going to stay in this bad relationship any more. It was the best breakup of my life. Ultimately, out of extreme despair comes extreme strength. And it proved especially true for us this time."

And he did leave. Over the coming months, he worked hard to make a new life for himself, and he didn't sever the bonds with his mother. He checked in on her and gave her whatever money he could to help with her expenses. This amazing boy-child-man knew in his heart it was his responsibility to take care of her. And he did, until she died of lung cancer from smoking.

The experience of working and meeting people who weren't in the same type of situation made him realize there are good people in the world, and he learned to benefit from their support and guidance. He had new role models and a new direction.

A year after Christopher moved into that first apartment, he felt he needed to leave his friends behind. He was ready for the next step. He enrolled in continuation school at age seventeen and went on to college after he got his GED. He stopped associating with people who were holding him back.

"That was both the easiest and the hardest thing for me to do. I'm a very loyal person, and I want to help everybody. But I knew I couldn't help anyone until I helped myself."

Even recently, one of those old friends came back home and tried to reconnect with some of the guys, including Christopher. "I realized many of them had taken bad routes in life, and I backed away. They had made their choices and I had made mine; we no longer had anything in common."

His advice: "Don't worry about what others think about you. Focus on what you want. Replace bad role models with good role models."

Christopher made many choices over the years, but the milestone he is most proud of is the one he made at the age of sixteen when he made the decision to leave the motel and his mother. It was scary and took a lot of courage, but it was the beginning of everything wonderful that followed.

In 2000, Christopher bought his first house and has vowed never to be homeless again. He earned his master's degree the same year—not bad for someone who started out as a seventh-grade dropout. Today he teaches people to be *unstoppable*. He is married to the love of his life, and they recently adopted a son.

The value that has become his guiding light is honesty. In his youth, he lied, cheated, stole, and broke the law. Never again will Christopher compromise. When you meet him, you are captivated by his smile, his self-confidence, his charm, and his genuine interest in other people. He tells it like it is—but always with love in his heart.

Christopher exudes other values, core beliefs that include authenticity, compassion, determination, friendship, kindness, responsibility, and security.

No matter where we come from, what adversities we face, we each have within us the ability to rise above it all and rewrite the script of our life. A key thread in Christopher's story is his choice of friends. Surrounding yourself with toxic and destructive people holds you back. When you recognize that, associating with positive people who share your values propels you toward a better future.

Have you ever really thought about how friends come into your life? When we're children playing on the playground, we tend to gravitate to kids who live near us, maybe go to the same school with us, attend church with us, take the same classes, or enjoy the same things. We don't really choose our friends; they just sort of happen. Then, as we get older, we become more selective about the people we surround ourselves with. We look for people who think like we do, act like we do, sometimes even look like we do. But more importantly, it's really about what we have in common. We begin to ask ourselves:

"Can I trust this person?"

"Does this person really care about me?"

"Does this person really understand?"

"Does this person accept me for who I am?"

Friendships are often forged in adult life when we go to college. It's a whole new experience. You're not living at home with your own family and sleeping in your own bed. You're in a new environment, and you're seeking new relationships. Of course, the college, the university, and sometimes even the major you take all offer opportunities for new friendships.

If you join a sorority or a fraternity, those bonds last a lifetime. Over the course of four years, you spend a lot of time with those men or women, and an affinity, an unspoken code that you're going to support each other and help each other in your career aspirations, develops.

Those are all the positive sides of how and why we pick friends. But there is also the not-so-positive side, the negative side of friendship where either because of our insecurities or our inability to connect with people, we end up associating with people we call friends—but are they really friends?

Do these people truly have your best interests at heart? Do these people care about you, or are they using you? Are they trying to justify their own actions by having others support what they do and join in? This can be drinking, sex, drugs, illegal activities like theft, petty larceny—or worse.

I would challenge you to take a piece of paper and write down your five closest friends. You may not have five and that's fine, but up to five—and no more than five. These might be people in your life now or people who have been in your life for a long time. Even if you don't talk to them every day, week, or month, you know no matter what, they will have your back. You could call them in an emergency, you could call them when you have something exciting to share, you could call them when you have something sad to share. And they will care and they will be there and they will support you. They will do whatever it takes—they will get on a plane to be at your side, or give you money if you need it at that moment in time.

Now that you've identified your five closest friends, next to their names write down how and when you met them. When did they come into your life? Next to each name, write down what is it about this person that makes them so special to you. Here are some examples:

> This person has an amazing charisma.
>
> We both enjoy wind sailing and traveling the world.
>
> He is incredibly intelligent and challenges me in a way that nobody else does.
>
> She understands me and know things about me that no one else does.
>
> I can trust that when this friend gives me feedback, it's from the heart, it's honest, and it's intended to help me.

Now think back to the time when you knew this person was a good friend. Did you choose them or did they choose you?

The reason this is important is because when friends choose us, we become part of their world, and when we choose them, they become part of our world. Neither is right or wrong, but just a curious way to think about how our lifelong friendships come into being. It's the *why* of our friendship.

As you look back on your list of five, here's a tough question. Is it possible there is someone on that list you call a friend, but maybe you struggled in how to define that relationship? If you can't articulate what it is about them that makes them important to you, what adds value to your life, then is this individual really a friend? Maybe this person is merely an acquaintance or someone who came into your life for a purpose but no longer holds that treasured place as one of your best friends.

Perhaps there was only one face that appeared for you. Maybe you only have one best friend. There's nothing wrong with that, as long as that person serves you in a positive way.

Have you ever heard someone say something along the lines of "You know, until this happened, I thought I knew who my friends were. But people that I didn't even realize cared or understood were the first to step up, and the people who I thought were my friends who would be there, I never heard from."

Sadly, this happens more often than you think. If you've experienced this, it doesn't mean that person wasn't your friend. They simply may not have had the capacity to step up and give you what you needed at that time. Other people that don't know you as well might care about you and have the innate capacity to show up for others in a time of need.

We can admire those people. We can envy those people, but the truth is not all of us are hardwired that way. Not everyone will drop everything to go help someone in need. Is it a test of friendship, or is it something broader than that? It's really not about friendship at all; it's about making a choice: A human being needs something, and it's my responsibility as a fellow human being to help.

I think you know where we're going with this. That type of person has values that are clearly identified and so deeply ingrained in them that they know no other way to act. They instinctively help somebody who has been in a car wreck, run into a building in flames to save a child or a pet, be available when someone has had a loss or diagnosed with cancer, or volunteer just to listen.

It puts a different spin on this word *friendship*. Even if you never see or hear from them again, their actions were no less sincere and no less meaningful to you at the time.

Friends are like fine wine. When you care for them properly they age well . . . with you and for you. Choose wisely.

HEALTH

*Time and health are two precious assets
that we don't recognize and appreciate
until they have been depleted.*
Denis Waitley

THERE ARE MORE gyms and fitness centers today than ever before. Why, then, is the United States' population the heaviest it's ever been? We are fatter than any other country in the world because we have access to so much food. And unfortunately, a lot of the food we eat is not good for us.

We eat for convenience rather than health, so we go to McDonald's and get that Big Mac, Chicken McNuggets, and large Coke and drive on to our next appointment. We don't just order coffee anymore; we want it laced with syrup. Instead of cooking fresh vegetables, we stock our freezers with ready-to-nuke calorie-laden substitutes. And instead of eating a healthy breakfast, we toast a Pop-Tart as we rush out the door. The food may curb our hunger cravings, but the compound effect clogs our arteries and balloons our bodies. It happens slowly over time, until we wake up one day and realize we're shopping for "industrial size" clothing.

If you ever get the chance, watch the movie *Super-Size Me* featuring Morgan Spurlock. He did an experiment where he went on a "McDonald's only" diet for thirty days. He went to the doctor, got a baseline status of his blood work, weight, and general health status. For the next thirty days, for every single meal, he went to McDonald's and ate from their menu. At the end of the thirty days, he had gained almost twenty-five pounds, his cholesterol was through the roof, and his blood sugar was out of whack. He was lethargic, developed high cholesterol, and experienced strange bodily sensations as well as depression. His doctors were stunned by the rapid decline in his health. Despite their advice, he stuck to his plan for the full thirty days before he returned to his normal eating habits. He ultimately returned to his original weight, but it took him five months to lose twenty pounds and another nine months to lose the last four-and-a-half pounds.

The addendum to the movie is where it gets interesting. They did an experiment to compare the same types of food from different sources. They went to a deli in New York City and ordered a regular hamburger with fries using fresh ground beef and potatoes that were cut and fried on the premises. Then they ordered burgers and fries from four or five other fast-food establishments in New York City. They put each one under a bell jar with a glass lid to cover the food. One week later, the fresh hamburger and fries from the deli started to get moldy and green. Within two weeks, the food was nasty looking, like a lab experiment gone wrong, and it had to be thrown away.

The hamburger from McDonald's, Burger King, and the other fast-food establishments, looked no different than when they were put under the jar. After six weeks they still looked the same because of all the chemicals and preservatives added to the food. Have you ever cleaned out your car and found that stray French fry under your seat? Other than maybe being dried out and stiff, it still looked the same as the day you bought it.

The film was criticized and attempts were made to debunk the findings. But who can argue with the fact that if you eat five thousand calories a day for thirty days with no exercise or physical activity, it's not good for you? Yet this is the type of food that we are putting in our bodies and our children's bodies every day. What is it doing to you?

Clearly this is a choice, a seemingly simple one that we make every day. What do we buy, cook, and ingest day after day—and what is the compound effect on our bodies?

Reflections by Carol:

I have struggled with my weight since I was fourteen years old. I remember specifically when and how it happened. I dislocated my knee practicing for cheerleader tryouts and as a result found myself immobile and in a plaster cast that went from my thigh to my ankle. My snack of choice, for reasons that elude me now, was Gerber's Zwieback Toast. In between meals I would devour them with milk. When the box was empty, I would beg for a bowl of ice cream. With no meaningful exercise and a daily intake of empty calories, I gained twenty-five pounds in six weeks.

I did manage to lose half the weight after I was fully back on my feet, but that time had influenced my eating habits and cravings—and not for the better. Over the years I have lost weight, gained it back, and lost it again, but the tricky thing about dieting is that, when you stop, your body overcompensates. Every time I would lose ten pounds, fifteen would come back. When I lost fifteen pounds, twenty would come back. You can do the math. Over time, I was winning small battles but losing the war.

The vicious cycle is exacerbated by the fact that the more weight you gain, the less motivated you are to exercise. And the older you get, the harder it is.

I am embarrassed to admit that as smart as I am about some things, I have (until recent years) been stupid about my own health and well-being. I'm optimistic that it's not too late to get better form and function for this old body, but I wish I had made better choices thirty years ago.

Reflections by Alan:

We need to make better choices about what we eat. One of the things I recently started doing is eating the way I did when I was a teenager. Growing up, I lived near my grandmother, and she had several gardens. We raised our own cattle. Until I went away to college, I really didn't eat that much fast food. Mostly my diet consisted of fruits and vegetables grown in our own garden. We cooked our own beef, and we had a little bit of chicken here and there. During that time, I had no weight problems. Of course, I was younger and more active too. As I got older, I started eating more and more fast food, and my weight started going up.

Recently my weight reached a point where I knew I had to make some changes. At some point, I came to the realization that I wasn't eating for nutrition; I was eating for convenience. So I started eating more fruits and vegetables and less fast food and drinking less soda pop and a lot more water. The changes have not been drastic or fast, but they are changes for the better. I feel more energetic. I sleep better. And my thinking is clearer.

My son Jesse is studying to become a personal trainer. He has helped me with strength training exercises that build muscle. He also said something I think is profound: "Abs are made in the kitchen, not the gym. Crunches, for the most part, don't work."

Another trainer friend of mine said weight loss is 80 percent food and 20 percent exercise. Instead of running on the treadmill for thirty minutes, eat two hundred less calories. Yes, exercise is important. However, food has a faster and longer-term effect on our weight.

Experts say we eat emotionally. We eat when we're stressed, when we're nervous, or when we're having a bad day. When those things happen, some people don't just eat—they tend to overeat. Can you recall the last time you sat in front of a television and finished off an entire pizza or ate a quart of ice cream?

Sometimes you just want to eat and get it out of your system. But you can't do that every day and expect to be healthy. Our work habits can have a negative influence on our eating too. We are pressed for time and focused on making money or boosting our career. In the process, we order takeout, eat at our desks or in our cars, and sacrifice healthy eating for unhealthy feasts.

As we get older, everything catches up with us. And sadly, if we don't find the power to change, we can't fix the problem. As Larry Winget says, "Your situation will improve right after *you* improve." When it comes to health, too many people will not try to fix a problem until it's almost too late. You've had a heart attack, a mini stroke, or your blood sugar is prediabetic. You know that if you don't do something soon, you're going to be in real trouble—you could even die.

Here's a sobering thought: Many people spend their entire lives sacrificing their health to gain wealth, but when they get older, they give away their entire wealth trying to get their health back.

Reflections by Alan:

Many years ago, I had the opportunity to meet the comedian Louie Anderson in Las Vegas. During his stand-up show, he made a comment that when he was a young comedian he hung out with people who liked to party. He said that during those times, he thought he was invincible, that he was never going to die. He would party with his friends every night. They would smoke. He would smoke. They would drink. He would drink. They would get high. He would get high. All to chase a thrill and discourage the boredom.

I remember him saying something like, "We would take drugs and do all these crazy things, more or less trying to kill ourselves. I finally woke up and stopped. Now that I'm older, I take pills and drugs trying to stay alive." Funny how we get wiser when we get older, but sometimes it's too late.

One of the men I work with was told by his doctor that he needed to lose weight or he was in for some big trouble. He is a very tall man and carried his weight well, so he didn't really look overweight. But because of his health concerns and having a young family to support, he changed his eating habits and limited his calorie intake by eating the proper foods. In the course of a year, he lost over one hundred pounds and kept it off. And . . . he *never* went to the gym.

Tim Walsh, a friend of mine, told me he was a typical gorger. He would sit down, eat twelve hot dogs at once, and think nothing of it. But his weight started to go higher and higher. He went to the doctor one day, and the doctor didn't give him good news. He said, "If you don't change your eating habits for the better and make some changes, you're going to die." He realized that the doctor was right. He stopped living that lifestyle. It wasn't easy, but he started running. He started eating more vegetables, drinking more water. He cut out a lot of sugar in his diet. Within three months, he lost fifty pounds. He set a goal to run a marathon in the Bahamas, which he did. He has been watching what he eats and running ever since. He's kept the weight off for over five years, feels much better, and knows he's probably going to live longer because of these lifestyle changes. He's now an advocate for healthier living. It's not that hard. It's just a matter of making choices. The right choices.

You don't have to go it alone. Making an appointment with your doctor for an annual physical is a great way to stay on top of the indicators. The patterns show up if your cholesterol, A1C sugar levels, or blood pressure are headed in the wrong direction. But our physical well-being doesn't end with better eating habits alone.

Exercise—yes, that dreaded word—is essential if you really want to move the needle on your health. It's easier than you think. Just get up and move! Sure, the optimal benefits may come from joining a gym, training for a marathon, or hiring a personal trainer. But if you're not ready for any of that, you can take control yourself and start doing little things that stack up to big results. Here's our challenge to get started:

1. Get off the couch and walk in place for five minutes while you're watching TV.
2. Stretch your arms and legs alternately, using a chair or a wall for support.
3. Park at the far end of the lot when you go to the grocery store or work.
4. Begin and end each day with deep breathing exercises. (This is ridiculously simple, and that puts it in the "no excuses" column.)

Here's the magic of exercise: A little bit leads to a little more, and a little more leads to meaningful change. We're all about choices, so just stop before you order your next meal and ask yourself, "Is this what I really want to put in my body?" And take a stand when it comes to exercise (pun intended).

MONEY MATTERS

You can be young without money,
but you can't be old without out it.
TENNESSEE WILLIAMS

DID YOU KNOW that money has been around for over one thousand years? The formal official use of money originated in China. By modern definition, it is used as a way to pay for goods and services. Money is the one thing in life that can cause or aggravate every emotion imaginable—from exhilarating joy to deep depression. And by the way, those extremes can apply to people who have lots of money or none at all. Money is something we use to function in our society. We use it to pay the rent or the mortgage, utility bills, groceries, and clothing, and buy indulgences that are important to us.

With money, it's all about how you choose to use it. And this is tied directly to how you value money. Some people either consciously or subconsciously feel that money is there to serve their needs, and they never worry about it. They know they can always make more, find more, use more, and spend more. They tend not to save. Those who see money as security tend to live more frugal lives. They make a choice to never live beyond their means and save every penny they can, whether it's for a rainy day or a specific goal such as buying a car or a house, sending the kids to college, or planning for retirement.

How do you value money? Have you always had money, or has money always been a struggle for you? When you don't have money to spend, when you can't afford to go out for that extra dinner, how does that make you feel? When you go into a store and try on a new dress or a new pair of shoes, and then look at the price tag and say to yourself, "I really can't afford this," what happens next?

What is the why behind not being able to afford something? It might be that you simply don't have the money—you don't make enough. You don't have enough disposable income for this particular purchase. It could be that you already have credit card debt, and you don't want to add to that. Maybe underneath what you're really saying is that you don't really need this; it might be a luxury that's completely unnecessary.

All of these are choices. But the values go beyond the value of money. They can touch on things such as the value of prestige, the value of status, or how you value your own security. So the real issue here is not money per se. Money is a means to an end. If it were only about the money, people would sit around with piles of cash and coins on their dining rooms tables, stuffed in their mattresses, and filling their pockets.

For many, money simply equals freedom! But money is really just a tool that represents what you can do with it, what you can buy with it, what you can acquire, what you can accumulate. Begin to think of money as an asset that can grow assets.

What are the assets that mean something to you? If you're living paycheck to paycheck and struggling to pay the rent, the car payment, buy food, and have clothes to wear, chances are you are not thinking about how that money could grow for you.

If you work for a company that provides some type of retirement savings plan or a 401K, you are encouraged to put a percentage of your paycheck into that every week or two—however you get paid. But for many people, that may be very difficult because that extra five, ten, or twenty dollars could mean keeping the lights on each month.

But as we grow and mature, our capacity and even our willingness to work to earn a living diminishes. The way our society is built, we're expected to somehow save enough money or invest and grow enough assets so we can take care of ourselves as we reach retirement age. For some, that can come in the form of investments in stocks or bonds. Maybe it's something much simpler than that for you—i.e., a savings account or CD that earns interest—but it's still money we don't touch. Maybe you like tangible things to invest in: real estate, gold, diamonds, paintings, or artwork. You may or may not enjoy these things physically—they might be stored away in a safety deposit box. Just knowing your investments are there is a form of security for you.

We put money into insurance policies; life insurance usually begins with the thought of taking care of your family and final arrangements at the time of your death. But life insurance can also return retirement earnings. If real estate is your game, do you invest only in your primary home, or do you have a second home? Maybe you use money for real estate investment-type properties—rental properties that will not only earn income for you now but also down the road when you sell them.

As you are thinking about how you relate to money and what choices you make, you'll find that it's not just what money can do for you now, but what money will mean and represent to you in the future.

We make a choice every day about how we treat people: how we greet them; how we respond and react to them; how we support or reject them. When was the last time you stopped to ask yourself before interacting with another person, "I wonder what's going on in his (or her) life right now"? Most of us are so caught up in our own agendas that we make choices to do or say things that matter only to us. Perhaps if we made a habit of taking a split second to see from the other person's perspective, what may have precipitated a situation or an attitude, we might make better choices on how to respond and as a result have more positive encounters.

The story we're going to share next is one that is reported far too frequently on the evening news: road rage. Road rage is a choice. It's a physical, emotional, visceral reaction to something that upset us based on someone else's actions on the road, and it can be deadly. There is an enormous difference between muttering under our breath about inconsiderate drivers and taking aggressive action against them.

Nathan's story has two parts. In the first part he was the hunter, and in the second he was the hunted. His relationship with money is at the core of his story.

Nathan is a very gregarious, successful industrial salesman; he's on the road five days a week because he covers a large geographic territory. Nathan finds that he can drive, get to his destination, and be very productive using mobile technology. While driving, he makes phone calls, sends text messages, answers emails, and even makes notes on the writing pad he keeps on the passenger seat beside him. He admits they are distractions and even illegal in many states. But Nathan describes himself as an experienced, safe driver who is able to multitask. "I didn't become the highest awarded salesperson in my company by wasting time. My drive time is my most valuable time to do all the administrative things I need to do in between appointments," he says.

During our conversation, it was clear that Nathan is exceedingly competitive. He never wants to lose a sale. And by his own admission, that competitiveness and relentless drive for the next sale is what precipitated his first road rage incident.

The day started out poorly. It began with a new client he had worked months to get an appointment with. The meeting lasted only five minutes when the owner stood, extended his hand toward the door, and told Nathan, "Thank you for your time. I'm not interested." Nathan was dismissed.

When he returned to his car, his phone buzzed. There was a message from his office that one of his biggest accounts was cancelling their business. To Nathan, this client represented annual income of over $30,000. While the loss of one client wasn't going to break the bank, the loss of the account represented more than the money. He considered the owner a friend, and he was insulted and hurt because the client had not called him first. "I was completely blindsided, and after just being kicked out of the earlier appointment, it put me over the edge." This volatile cocktail of emotions, including confusion, frustration, anger, along with loss of personal control, was the incendiary device that put him on the collision course to what happened next.

He started his car, and as he left the parking lot, the details churned in his mind. He rationalized the failed appointment and vowed to himself things would go differently the next time. He switched his attention to the lost client. He knew that a competitor had been vying for this business for a long time. In fact, he knew the salesman, because they often ran into each other on the road. His rival was also aggressive and could be very charming. Nathan couldn't deny this competitor had a good product to sell, but he never imagined the client would dump him in favor of the other company. After all, he gave them the best pricing and provided prime service. He didn't yet know any of the facts behind the decision, but his internal fabrication fueled the anger convulsing in his gut. "The other salesman's face appeared like a mirage, and every fiber of my being wanted to hunt him down and punch his lights out for stealing my business."

Without even realizing it, Nathan had driven thirty miles and was coming into the city where his office was located. It was close to the noon hour, and traffic was heavy. Generally, he was not a "lane changer," but the car in front of him was driving too slow, even for the conditions. The woman behind the wheel had plenty of room to close the gap between her and the car in front of her. She didn't need to ride her brake. If he could get her to move over, he could get back to his office faster and try to fix this mess.

He pulled up on her bumper, flashed his lights, honked his horn, and shouted obscenities along with the customary hand signals. There was nowhere for her to go due to the high volume of cars.

Then the traffic ahead stopped. She stopped, but Nathan didn't. He slammed her from behind and forced her car to graze the concrete median before coming to a stop. Due to the reduced speed they had been traveling, Nathan's air bag didn't deploy. He unfastened his seat belt and jumped out of his car, still screaming obscenities. "Who taught you to drive, you crazy bitch?"

The lady opened her door and attempted to stand. She appeared to be in her mid-fifties, dressed in a tailored business suit. She turned and looked up at Nathan with tears streaming down her face, gasping for breath. Nathan caught her just before her head hit the ground. He propped her against the door. "My anger just vaporized, and I dialed 911." It only took a few minutes for the police to respond. They gave the woman oxygen while they waited for the paramedics.

Nathan was standing a few feet away, giving the police his statement, when he overheard her say to the EMT, "I have to get to the hospital. I'm fine; don't worry about me. My husband had a heart attack at work, and they're waiting for me."

Nathan said this was a life-changing moment for him. "My own anger could have caused the death of another human being—and for no reason." He had only seen an older woman as a slow, annoying driver standing between him and his destination.

"I realized in that moment that I had no idea what was going on with that driver. I had no idea the pain that she was in, the reason why she was on the road, and the importance of her getting to her destination safely."

Nathan was charged with reckless driving. His insurance had to pay for the damage to both cars and he got two points on his driving record.

Nathan continued with his story. "I'd like to say I was a changed man. I did get better for a while, but the truth is, as time went on I allowed that competitive impulse to creep back into my driving. I never had another accident, but I suppose I could have. It wasn't until a couple years later when I had a health scare of my own that I truly changed my life and my driving.

"As I lay in the hospital after my heart attack, I thought about that woman's husband and recalled her slumping to the ground in tears. It was only then that I took full responsibility for my role in causing that accident. I was done with obsessing over my bank account; life was passing me by and I had come face-to-face with death."

Nathan reflected on how he and other people he knows in similar high-pressure jobs go through life rationalizing their actions. Maybe it's the thrill of the sale; maybe it's the drive for money; sometimes it's the lust for recognition. "Making self-centered choices without regard to their impact on other people always ends badly. I knew I had to change. I wanted to become a better person. I needed to make better choices."

Nathan started eating healthier, exercising every day, and began devoting weekend time to support fund-raising efforts for a local community project. "My business and career were doing well. I was still successful, but I no longer chased the trophy. I found my rhythm and realized that I didn't have to be such a lunatic about closing the next sale."

Nathan met his wife during one of those fund-raising drives. Today they have two children, ages two and four. Now when Nathan gets behind the wheel, the images of his wife and children keep him centered, and he no longer uses his drive time to text. "I found out I could drive the speed limit (well, maybe five miles over the speed limit); I could choose a lane and stay there; and if there was someone behind me wanted to go faster, it wasn't a sign of weakness to pull over and let them pass."

Nathan wasn't prepared for what came next, however. He was driving to have lunch with one of his regular clients. He ran into the same type of congested traffic that existed on the day of his accident. Traffic was moving slowly, but cars were still changing lanes to get ahead. Nathan he remembered thinking, *You know, they don't get it. They don't understand that nothing is that important, and they're not really going to get there faster.*

"I wasn't paying attention to the car in my rearview mirror. And by the time I realized how closely the driver was tailgating me, he had started flashing his lights and honking his horn. I looked for my opportunity to move over, but it didn't come quickly because tractor trailers and cars merging from the right lane to the center lane. I found my opening and moved to the middle lane, and the car behind me followed. My gut told me to get off the highway and out of his way. I moved again to the right and prepared to get off at the next exit. It was only a quarter mile, but my tailgater was still following close behind. As I eased onto the exit ramp, I breathed a sigh of relief because it looked like he was going to stay on the highway. But as I slowed down and he passed, his passenger window rolled down, and the last thing I remember was seeing the gun a second before the blast and feeling searing pain."

According to the police report, Nathan's car spun out of control, hit the guardrail, and flipped on its side. Witnesses had reported seeing a black car tailgating Nathan, but the car was never found and driver the was never caught. The shot missed his heart by a fraction of an inch, but Nathan suffered a collapsed lung, multiple fractures and contusions, and spent three months in a rehabilitation center.

"I'm here to tell the story because I didn't die—but I could have. It's kind of ironic that the guy who was the hunter had become the hunted."

I asked Nathan what he would say if he could talk to his younger self. "That's easy. I would tell him to make the right choices in life—choices that respect other human beings and don't violate laws. I finally figured out that the Golden Rule my grandmother used to preach wasn't so corny after all. And common sense serves us better than ignorance or stupidity. The next sale is not worth it; the impact on other people is not worth it; the price you pay in life is not worth it."

What values can we see reflected in Nathan's story? According to him, his values haven't changed. What has shifted is their intensity and balance. Nathan's core values include determination, achievement, and recognition. Earlier in life they were all-consuming and completely self-centered. He says, "I always thought that if I kept my eye on those three things, I could achieve anything, and the truth is, I did . . . but at a price. I have learned through these experiences that I unwittingly added three words in parentheses after each word: *at any cost.*"

Nathan has not lost his personal desire for determination, achievement and recognition. Those things are still important to him. What has changed is the "at any cost." Perhaps the question we should be asking ourselves is: "Do I have values that are being stretched or justified because of a caveat I have attached—a means to an end?"

Reflections by Alan:

Money, finances, capital—whatever you call it, we all want it, and we want *more* of it. So how do we make more money? More importantly, how do we *keep* more money? To explain further I am going to share some very commonsense advice I learned both from my parents and from Jim Rohn. As you have noticed, Jim Rohn is mentioned several times in this book. Jim was an Idaho farm boy who became involved in a business opportunity and did well financially. Over the years, he was asked to share his philosophies on life. Most of his information is common sense, biblically based, and involves tried and true methods. Thankfully, I had the opportunity to meet Jim Rohn twice before he died in 2009. He was a true gentleman.

Until you are either trained or educated in a specific field of work, you essentially are a commodity, meaning that you have no specific skills. This does not mean you aren't a valuable person. You are very valuable to your family and friends, but that is not why the market (job) pays you. There is a lot of talk in the news today about people working in the fast-food industry who want the minimum wage to be fifteen dollars per hour or higher. There are political and philosophical leanings from both sides explaining why this is either good or bad depending on your viewpoint. We are not here to argue that. If the local economy can handle fifteen dollars per hour wages, then great! Someone who works in fast food making fifteen dollars per hour working forty hours per week would earn just over $31,000 in a year. Not bad. But remember roughly 30 percent will be taken out for taxes, social security, benefits, etc., so this person will end up bringing home about ten dollars per hour, or about $22,000 a year. Not bad, especially if you have never made any significant money, but try to support a family, buy a car, pay off student loans, go on vacation, own a smartphone, pay rent, and buy food. I promise you won't get very far on those wages.

But why would you want to stay in a minimum wage job for very long anyway? What you need to know is that companies pay you to perform specific tasks, fix things, or solve problems. The bigger the problems you can solve, the more money you can earn usually. That's where education (the right kind), training, and experience all come into play. We were not designed to be mediocre. We are designed to reach our full potential, and that is what we should strive for.

Jim suggests the 70/30 rule, which is a very simple plan. Whatever amount of money you bring home, learn to live on 70 percent of that. If you brought home two thousand dollars per month, learn to live on fourteen hundred. It's difficult for sure, but you must start somewhere. The 30 percent or six hundred dollars that you haven't spent should be used in three other areas. First, give 10 percent or two hundred dollars to charity. That can be your church or an organization that promotes a cause you believe in. Second, the next 10 percent should be invested in some sort of vehicle to create wealth—stocks, bonds, business investment, etc. This money is to be used to make money. The last 10 percent should be saved. This is your rainy-day fund for when the car breaks down, the air conditioner conks out, or the kids need braces. The key is to take that 30 percent out first and live on the rest. If you can follow those guidelines when you *aren't* making much money, it will pay huge dividends later when you *are* making good money.

Recently I read a book titled, *Me, Inc.* by Gene Simmons. Yes, *that* Gene Simmons of the rock group KISS. The book was rich with information about his upbringing and his work ethic. Now, I will admit I was never a huge KISS fan, and I always kind of judged him for his rock star lifestyle. However, after reading this book, I'm very impressed with the amount of hard work, dedication, and business savvy he has. Gene Simmons achieved his success through serious hard work and knowing what he wants. If we all followed his work ethic example, we would all be successful.

One of the things I have seen over the years in the younger generations (including myself looking back) is that they all want it *now*! Young people want the big house, the fancy vacations, the nicer cars, the big-screen TVs, the smartphones, the computers—the stuff their parents have, but they want it now without investing the years necessary to earn the money to acquire it. So they get a credit card (or two or three or twelve). Credit cards can be very useful and can get us out of a bind in a pinch, but we should not rely on them as a way to support our everyday operations or prematurely indulge our wish list.

It is important to have good credit, and you have to start somewhere. But keep in mind that your credit rating is used for more than just seeing if you are credit worthy. Insurance companies, employers, and many other institutions look at your credit rating to help determine if they will do business with you and/or how much they may charge you for their services. When you decide to purchase a home with a mortgage, you will need to have some credit established. This can be accomplished in many ways, including having a basic credit card (i.e., Visa, MasterCard, etc.) or getting a car loan or a personal loan. The credit companies want to see how you handle your debts. Keeping your debt-to-credit ratio at 30 percent or less is ideal. This means that if you have a credit line of $10,000 through two or more credit cards, keep the overall balance under $3,000.

People get into trouble when they use credit cards for everyday purchases. It is much easier to pay with plastic than cash because there is no real pain involved—until the monthly statement comes in the mail. After you open the envelope, there may be real pain as you look at the statement and realize you forgot about making over half of those purchases, and they all add up! If possible, use cash whenever you can. I recently purchased a used car, and the gentlemen I was negotiating with lowered his price because I told him I had cash available to buy the car on the spot. The other person who was interested in the car needed to get a loan. The old saying "cash is king" is still true today.

We all need money to function in society. We all know how to spend money; the trick is to learn how to earn money. Learn how to save money, and learn how to invest money. Become more valuable in the marketplace by increasing your skills and knowledge to solve those bigger problems. Learn to say no to those impulsive purchases that end up in the junk drawer anyway. If you spend a little time paying attention to money, it will serve you well in the future.

Reflections by Carol:

I have never been a good saver. I have never lived beyond my means, but I made a habit (for years) of living right up *to* my means. Don't get me wrong; I have good insurance, I've invested some over the years, and I always contributed to the 401K. But I also always did just enough to satisfy my guilt that I needed to put something away for my future.

Because my father was a young man at the time the Great Depression hit, his ultra-conservative attitudes about money and security overwhelmed me, and there was that little bit of rebellion that surfaced when money was involved. I didn't want to deny myself what I wanted if I could afford it.

When I was in my twenties, I made that fatal mistake of having and using too many credit cards. I was in deep and smart enough to know that paying the minimum every month was not the solution to get out of debt. I was lucky. I found a legitimate lender who granted me a consolidation loan so I could pay off all the cards with only one payment a month. The interest rate was higher than normal, but it didn't break any usury laws.

It took me two years to pay everything off. During that time, I closed all of the department store accounts except my Sears card, and I kept only one MasterCard. I even took a course on money management and put a system in place that allowed me a limited amount of spending for discretionary items like new clothes or dining out. It was painful, but the new habits stuck with me from that point forward.

But that was then, and this is now. Looking back, the question I should have been asking myself was "What will my financial situation be when I am ready to retire?" The plan that I should have put in place for the time I would no longer want to or be able to work was nonexistent. I didn't think I'd be working forever, but I also didn't seriously consider the number of years I would have to support myself with no meaningful income.

My story actually has a happy ending. I finally figured it out in my fifties and made the necessary changes in my investments and my savings to know that my future is secure. This is not what I would recommend to others, though.

If I had made better choices and put a higher value on money and the essential role it plays in our later years, I would be in an even stronger position today.

The bottom line is that money plays a critical role throughout our lives. It covers our essential living expenses, allows us to indulge in our wants (not just needs) from time to time, and it must be there when the paychecks stop coming.

As you think about your own circumstances and how you value money, we encourage you to fast-forward into the future. What will your needs be? What resources will you have to draw upon? What will happen if there is a catastrophic event that depletes your reserves? Is there someone in your life who will share in the responsibility of paying bills, medical costs, long-term care, and even your final expenses?

A shift in how you think about money today will give you peace of mind as you grow older. Make that choice to secure your future.

PERSONAL

*It is our choices . . . that show
what we truly are,
far more than our abilities.*
J. K. ROWLING

SOMETIMES WHEN WE are faced with important choices, we want to change our lives. We want to change our personal situation. We want to change our job or careers or maybe even where we live. For most people this doesn't happen in an instant. It's something we think about, something we dream about. Dreams are very often the precursor to making those choices. Tapping into that vision of what you want your life to be, what it could or should be, is very exciting. We paint vivid pictures, and we fantasize about what's going to happen.

But the difference between dreamers and doers comes down to the word *choice*. Dreaming is important, and we should never stop dreaming. But until you take action—until you make a choice to do something to move yourself forward—it's nothing but a dream. It's not a reality, and it's never going to get you from where you are to where you want to be.

Are you a doer or a dreamer? I find when I'm around fellow entrepreneurs, the paradox between dreamers and doers becomes extremely evident. You could line people up against two walls. On the left side are the people who have unbelievably vivid and exciting dreams, and then you see them six months or a year later, maybe even five years later, and they're still talking about those same dreams. The details may have faded, or they may be more vivid. Maybe the dream has morphed into version two or three, but it's still only a dream. Nothing has fundamentally changed.

On the right side are the people who shared a dream with you, and when they leave that room, walk out of that seminar, conference, or event, they leave with a purpose to turn that dream into reality They have made a choice to take a decisive action, that first step to move toward the realization of their dream.

It is not an easy thing to do. It's much easier just to dream about it, think about it, or fantasize about it. You might work out all the details in your head, but something holds you back from taking action. Is it fear? And if it is, is it fear of success or fear of failure? Are you concerned about how your dream is going to impact your family, your children, your spouse, your friends?

Maybe you hold back because you talk yourself out of it. You laugh it off. "Oh, it was just a dream. I don't have the time. I don't have the resources. I don't have the expertise." You know what? Time, resources, and expertise can all be obtained if you make a choice to go after them. And that often is what stops people. They are so clear about what their goal will be like when the football goes between the two posts for that extra point, but they haven't worked out the plays that are going to get them down field. How are they going to get another two yards? Another four yards? Avoid an interception? Not get tackled? Get another first down?

When you watch football, the crowd roars when the quarterback throws a fifty or sixty-yard pass and a receiver catches it and runs it into the end zone. It's very exciting. But when we're trying to make choices in our life to change things, change a pattern, change our circumstances, change our financial situation, it isn't a single dramatic play. It's usually not even a straight line. There are going to be a lot of zigs and zags. There will be unforeseen obstacles that pop up when you least expect them. Sticking with football as our metaphor, there are going to be others that try to intercept or take you down along the way. The commitment to your dream, the commitment to make it to the end zone, should be with the understanding and belief that there are going to be a lot of small choices along the way that will get you there.

You've probably heard the phrase, "Eat an elephant one bite at a time." It's kind of a silly phrase, but there's a lot of truth in it. You could never sit down and eat an entire elephant at one sitting even if you wanted to—you must start with one bite. Moving toward big shifts in our lives or monumental change is exactly like eating the elephant. It's a series of small choices (small bites), and when you break them down, it really becomes a lot easier because when you make one choice and it moves you to the next step, you are encouraged to make another choice and another choice and another choice. And along the way you will be touching base with your values. You will ask yourself, "Is this still important to me? Am I on the right path? Do I have the right vision, or should I adjust my plan?" But no matter where you end up, it's going to be different and most likely better than where you are right now. That's when choices become exciting.

In this way you are empowering yourself to make the choices that are right for you. And you are also empowering yourself to make different choices, to change the route, to change the goal, to move the end zone, and that's OK—because it's *your* life. But if you are sitting at the opposite end of the stadium in the stands, looking way down the field at that far end zone, and all you do is dream and never get on the field, nothing will change. And that's a choice too. Is doing nothing for this particular goal the right choice for you?

Reflections by Carol:

This book is not meant to be philosophical. When I was in college, though, I took philosophy and read Kant, Plato, Aristotle, Socrates, Nietzsche, Descartes, and one particular quote by Rene Descartes has always stuck with me. I think it applies here. The quote was "I think, therefore I am."

"I think, therefore I am"—what does that mean to you? As human beings, we have the ability to think. Is this the essence of our being? That's where you get into the philosophical debate of what life is all about. But I want to apply his quote in a slightly different way here. By thinking about those things going on in your life right now—your relationship with money, your relationship with your spouse or partner, your children, your friends, your spirituality, whatever the category—as you think about those things and they become integrated into your life, your thought process will lead you to choices. Whether they are spur of the moment or well-planned, well-thought-out choices really doesn't matter, because all of them started with a thought.

I think therefore I am. And the fact that *I am* gives me power over the choices I make, the values I associate with, believe in, and live by, and ultimately my perfect life.

Why would a doctor give up private practice to work in a federal penitentiary? Dr. Susan Mowatt's story will be told in the first person. She spoke at a recent event at our local library, and the following is the script she used to tell her inspiring story of growing up, the challenges she faced, and the choices she made.

"I grew up in the mountains of Northeastern Pennsylvania, the third of four children in a relatively traditional middle-class family. My parents married as teenagers, and although they often struggled to make ends meet, we had all of what we needed and most of what we wanted.

"My mother was and still is very maternal. Her life revolved completely around family and she instilled strong family and religious values. My father, ambitious and fun-loving, worked hard and played hard. In either case, he was seldom home. Despite the family denial that continued until well after his fatal heart attack in 1982 at the age of thirty-seven, my father was an alcoholic. He and my mother were separated at the time of his death, and it was not until my early twenties when I began attending ACOA (Adult Children of Alcoholics) meetings that I was able to begin to understand issues such as codependency and how those issues affected me personally.

"Although I did not inherit my mother's peacemaking skills or her ability to 'smile through it all,' I do attribute my determination to her. My attributes from my father are a good sense of humor, high energy, and an all-or-nothing attitude, which for the most part have served me well.

"A good work ethic was instilled in me by both my parents. At the age of eight, I started with an early morning paper route. The holidays were the worst because the papers were extra heavy. It was dark, cold, and the wind would be howling, and I would go into my parents' bedroom to see if my mom would drive me, and my father would say 'get going.' And off I would go into the pitch black. (I am being a little melodramatic, but not much!)

"I then took a job babysitting a local pediatrician's family at the ripe old age of eleven, leaving delivery of newspapers behind. One of the children I cared for was a hemophiliac. Because of exposure to his illness and an understanding that his body did not have enough Factor VIII, I began recruiting people to donate blood to the Red Cross. I should tell you it was difficult to get people to donate back then. Factor VIII could not be manufactured; it required blood donations. It was necessary to pool many specimens to get enough Factor VIII, therefore many hemophiliacs were exposed to infectious diseases such as hepatitis and HIV. This young boy relied on frequent transfusions so as not to bleed into his brain or his joints. It was not unusual for him to be in a lot of pain, and his mother, a nurse, educated me on meditation exercises to assist him in relaxation and imagery, and he found relief in a whirlpool-like tub.

"One night while I was watching him and his brother, he needed to get in the tub for water therapy. I removed the safety helmet that he wore constantly while he was out and about because of his rambunctious personality. His brother was more mild-mannered and quiet; he enjoyed reading and sitting still.

Brook, on the other hand, was adventurous and always a moving target. This particular night he got out of the tub and promptly fell down a flight of stairs. I was horrified—I thought he was going to die. I called his parents and upon their arrival home we gave him a transfusion right there in the kitchen. This horrible accident was the spark that pushed me to pursue a career in medicine.

"Many other jobs would follow. I made pizza and ice cream on Main St. at Smith's in Hawley, Pennsylvania, during high school. While in college I cleaned movie theaters, worked the Rocky Horror Picture Show on Wisconsin Ave. in Washington, D.C. I waited tables, did room service, and hauled brick and block for the construction of million-dollar homes. I was also a nanny to several children while in college, and the mother of the family sat me down at the end of my tenure with her and gave me some advice that I will never forget. 'Be very careful of the career you choose or your children may end up behaving like mine and seeking out their nanny when they are hurt, afraid, happy, or getting ready for bed.'

"I also had the opportunity to provide assistance to a ninety-three-year old woman who had escaped Nazi Germany. In exchange for a studio apartment (which during the eighties was worth about seven hundred dollars a month.) I took her to the doctor, did laundry, and walked with her every day. She taught me more than I could ever relay to you here. She made me slow down and enjoy nature and all it had to offer. She taught me to be more frugal. We would go to the grocery store, and she would make me gather the loose grapes and take them to the grocer to be priced. She stated that if she 'did not do this, the grapes would be wasted' and besides, she 'could get a large bag of grapes off the vine for about fifteen cents.'

"In the fall of 1985, I entered nursing school at Georgetown University in a special double-track program. The purpose of the program was to provide the graduate with a nursing degree as well as the requisites for medical school entrance. My plan was that, if I decided I did not want to go to medical school, I would have a career as a nurse, and if I decided to move on, I could do that as well. I was always trying to keep my options open. While the incorporation of premed courses into the nursing curriculum worked well in theory, it was nearly impossible in practice due to the heavy scheduling conflicts. Upon entering my junior year, I realized I was not going to have all the courses I would need to apply to medical school. In order to take the remainder of requirements needed for medical school, it necessitated the Dean of the College of Arts and Sciences to accept me in transfer from the School of Nursing. I therefore set up a meeting with the Dean of Nursing. I explained my situation—the need to complete certain classes, scheduling conflicts, etc.—and I was contemplating transferring to the College of Arts and Sciences. She responded, 'Do you think you have what it takes to be a physician?'

"I often wonder if she knew me well enough that she was trying to push me to prove that I did, or if she really thought I could not achieve my goals. No matter. If I did not have the confidence in myself when I walked into that meeting, at the conclusion I certainly knew I could do it for no other reason than to *show her* I could. I transferred into the College of Arts and Sciences, extended my length of study to five years with a semester off to earn money to pay for the additional year of schooling.

"Upon graduation from college, I was offered a position doing breast cancer research at the Lombardi Cancer Center in Washington, D.C. I was reluctant and insecure about taking my MCAT exams and thought perhaps I would work a few years to pay down my educational debt. After two to three years, I realized it was time to go to medical school or pursue my PhD. I had very little interest in doing research for my career, so I informed my supervisor of my intention. Afterwards it seemed that my hours got longer instead of shorter. I again reiterated my desire to take the MCAT exam and stated that I needed to work only forty hours a week in order to spend some time in preparation. The lead investigator did not want me to leave my post. Concurrently, my grandmother had fallen ill at home, so I left my job in D.C. to return to Hawley once more.

"I started to bartend at night at Pat's Bar (5:00 p.m. to 2:00 a.m.), and during the day (6:00 a.m. to 3:00 p.m.) I painted houses. Later I was offered a job assisting an elderly woman who was a retired schoolteacher in town. The combination of jobs enabled me to study some during the day, provide a service to Ms. Swingle, and be home to assist in any way I could with my grandmother. I studied hard. Test day was quickly approaching. I tend to be a pretty good test taker, but I have also been known to have a little 'black cloud' that follows me everywhere. The MCAT was being offered at the University of Scranton, and all I could envision was trying to drive to Scranton in the early morning hours, getting behind a truck, and somehow not getting there on time. The exam paperwork clearly stated that if you were late, you would not be granted access to the exam . . . no exceptions.

"Taking every precaution, I rented a hotel room the night prior to the exam. This would eliminate all potential obstacles, or so I thought. All I needed to do was get a good night's sleep before the exam. Little did I know that my room was located above the hotel bar and there was a bowling convention in town.

I called the front desk due to the loud music and explained that I had a very important exam in the morning and asked if it was possible to move my room to anywhere but above the bar. She politely said, 'I am very sorry but there are no rooms that I can move you into due to the bowling convention.'

"Feeling completely out of control, I did what every young person does in a moment of crisis—I called my mother. She could hear the stress in my voice and told me she would do anything she could to help me. I realized there was nothing either one of us could do, whimpered and said, 'I guess I will just put the pillow over my head and try to go to sleep.'

"After completing the test, the waiting began. Daily, I would ask my mailman, Mike (he is still my mailman), 'Anything for me?' and he would respond, 'No, not today.' Day after day, no response, until finally on a rainy afternoon my grades came. 'How'd ya do, kid?' In spite of the bowling convention shenanigans, I had done quite well.

"I was accepted into medical school at Penn State College of Medicine in Hershey, Pennsylvania and attended from 1994 to 1998. In the midst of medical school, I got married and inherited an immediate family; I returned to medical school in the fall of 1996 with three children, ages nine, eight, and six. In my last year, I was pregnant with my daughter while interviewing and traveling for residency programs.

"My daughter was born in Wayne Memorial Hospital, the same hospital both my husband and I were born in, during an incredible snowstorm at the end of 1997. She was born on December 29, so as luck would have it I was able to claim her on my taxes for the whole year!

"Match Day is in the spring, and that is when you rank programs and they rank you, and if they match, you have a position in their residency program. This too, was complicated since we had three children in school, and we were evaluating the different cost of living school programs and reputations, and ultimately the goal of an outstanding residency program. We set our sights on Williamsport Family Practice Residency Program for many reasons. My husband had studied at WACC, it was relatively close to home, and it offered obstetrics training without having to send the resident away for extended periods of time, thereby being separated from one's family.

"As luck would have it, we matched with Williamsport. We relocated there with the purchase of our first house, and then the work began. One hundred-hour work weeks, on call every third day for thirty-six hours at a clip. I participated in all kinds of rotations, including surgery, obstetrics, hospice, and ICU, and then, near the end of the second year of residency, my husband was diagnosed with testicular cancer. He had emergency surgery over Memorial Day weekend. At this time, we had four children, three from my husband's first marriage and our daughter.

"I continued to ask questions of God like, 'I am trying really hard here. Not sure what I have done to upset you, but this is ridiculous. What will I do if my husband does not survive? What about these kids? How will I finish residency and take care of them?' Well, we were fortunate. His treatment went very well, and against all odds we got pregnant with out last child, and I delivered a beautiful baby boy in February of 2001.

"Upon graduation, I was offered a position with the residency program as a full-time clinician but also a mentor and educator of residents. It was the culmination of lifelong aspirations. I was impacting impressionable residents and loving every minute of it. I thought we would stay there forever.

"After five years and the ever-changing landscape of medicine, I was told that our practice was going to increase our productivity in order to generate more revenue. I tried to ask them to cut my salary, increase my hours, but please, I needed more than fifteen minutes per patient. I approached those in leadership roles and was told, 'If you do not want to comply with these requirements, there is the door.'

"I took the door. I returned to my hometown and opened a solo practice and began living the dream. I opened my doors on Main Street in Dr. Pardine's old office where almost everyone I knew in Hawley had received care at one time or another. I later moved to 69 Church Street, a home where I delivered the dreaded morning newspaper so many years before. Keystone Family Practice was established October 2006 and closed in August 2014.

"Now, I know what you are thinking. Why would someone leave private practice in a quaint small town practicing old-fashioned country medicine to manage the delivery of medical care in a maximum-security prison?

"My decision to leave private practice was not an easy one to make. Medicine over the last twenty years has changed drastically. If someone approached me upon graduation from medical school and said I would be practicing in a maximum-security United States penitentiary for convicted male inmates, I would have said, 'What, are you kidding? Not me!' Let me enlighten you. Provided I was aware of how great an opportunity prison medicine was, I would be entering my last year of practice at the ripe old age of fifty-three.

"Let's talk about the obvious reasons people make decisions with regard to their career direction.

"Pay—I am making now a modest amount for a person in medicine. I more than doubled my salary by taking this position. Not that I am making so much money now; rather, I was making so little in private practice. On average, my reimbursement for a complicated medical patient was less than fifty dollars. I have always seemed to be in an office that was right next to a hair salon, and most women know you cannot get a cut and color for only fifty dollars.

"Hours—In private practice it was not uncommon to work seventy to eighty hours per week. That was not all direct patient care, but all that goes along with being self-employed: payroll, insurance postings, paying bills, negotiating contracts with insurance companies for better reimbursement, etc. People used to say to me, 'Why don't you hire an office manager to negotiate for you?' Oh my, why didn't I think of that? I would only need to pay them more than I am making, provide health insurance benefits and a retirement package. Yes. Why didn't I think of that?

"Health insurance—Let us juxtapose how much health insurance costs for the small local businessman or businesswoman. I was paying $1,600 a month for a healthy family of four. My position now takes five hundred dollars per month out of my pay for better coverage than I was able to afford on my own. Without getting into politics, most people who argue about health insurance for all Americans make assumptions that people are just looking for a handout. I was not looking for a handout, but falling on difficult economic times and decided to gamble with *not* having health insurance. Don't forget, that $1,600 was just for health insurance. I also needed malpractice insurance, and my exclusive rate since I had no cases on my record was a mere $20,000 a year. OK, so realistically, $20,000 for health coverage, $20,000 for malpractice, and about $20,000 to 25,000 for office space requires $65,000 before staff is paid and provided medical insurance coverage, workers compensation, etc. And by the way, at this point I had not yet been paid.

"Retirement—In private practice, since my earnings were meager to say the least, I never seemed to have enough to put toward my future. The Bureau of Prisons provides both a Thrift Savings Plan and a pension payable after as little as ten years with full retirement after twenty years. I will now be able to retire with a secure financial plan at the age of sixty-six for full retirement and as young as fifty-six with better financial security than I was able to provide being self-employed.

"The above represents some of the thoughts I pondered about prior to closing my practice, but it is certainly not inclusive. Let's add some substance that is unique to the practice of medicine.

"First, how does one get paid in medicine today? Productivity, of course.

In a family practice office, you are expected to see thirty-five to forty people per day. The workday is longer than eight hours in general, but the patient load is expected to be completed in an eight-hour day. That leaves 13.7 minutes per patient if you see thirty-five, or twelve minutes if you see forty. Again, this does not take into account people getting vitals, getting undressed, getting redressed—not much time to provide the type of care I was expecting to practice. In the prison, I see about ten to twelve patients per day, which allows me the luxury of educating, implementing, and evaluating all aspects of an individual's preventive medicine plan.

"Second, on the outside, this is the way I refer to medicine in the free world: Insurance companies control everything. The medication you can take, the testing that is approved or denied, what hospital you can go to, what rehab participates whether for drugs and alcohol or physical rehabilitation or psychologist or psychiatrist if mental health coverage is an option at all on your plan. The beauty of the Eighth Amendment of the Constitution is that facilities must provide medical care to inmates. I have the ability to practice good, solid medicine—everyone is on a level playing field; medical care is fair in prison. On the outside, the better your insurance, the better your care—God forbid you have medical assistance—you are then given substandard care because, after all, we are not earning any money on those people. Call something in; don't fill a slot with them when you can get a Blue Cross Blue Shield patient in that slot—after all, we are here to make money, aren't we?

"This is rationing health care, and it happens all the time. I am proud to say it did not happen in my office and perhaps was also a contributing factor to my demise. I am obligated by my Hippocratic Oath to do no harm. I have an ethical obligation to do the right thing when it comes to medicine. Do you have any idea what it feels like when you know the right thing to do and a clerk on the other end of the phone line, with zero medical training, says 'what are the symptoms of the young lady you want to do an MRI/MRA scan on?'

"Answer: 'Her father, her grandmother, and her paternal uncle all had aneurysms in the brain.'

"Response: 'I'm sorry, she has no symptoms.'

"My response: 'I AM TRYING TO SCREEN HER BEFORE SHE HAS SYMPTOMS!'

Symptoms with a brain aneurysm are often deadly, but of course this clerk has no understanding of that. She is just paid to deny scheduling such expensive tests.

"Third, some people say, 'I guess I just need to commit a heinous crime, and then you will continue to provide care for me.' Some are kidding; some are not. Those inmates are getting better care than some U.S. citizens who have not committed any crime.

"This sounds like we should be working harder to provide more sufficient care on the outside, not take away from those on the inside. If you want to go to prison for the great medical care, you also need to be told when to eat, what you eat, and be rationed toiletries whether or not you have a problem—i.e., ulcerative colitis and you are not eligible for toilet paper until the middle of the week. It is definitely *not* worth going to prison for the medical care. However, all the people I have left behind have options—these inmates do not.

"I truly do not expect everyone to agree with my decision, but anyone who knows me knows I try to live a good, godly life. I believe this job opportunity provides a better future for my family with regards to more time and financial security, and it provides me personally with an opportunity to serve the broken, those living on the fringe. It is quite humbling to work with people who have no choices about anything in their life. It has taught me about all I have to be grateful for. These inmates are just people, not the animals that so many try to convince others they are. Have they done terrible things? Yes, and a lot have done those things under the influence of drugs or alcohol.

"If I had not been born in Honesdale, Pennsylvania, with an intact family that valued education and hard work, would I be in the position I am today? I think not. There is no validity to equal opportunity in prison—many of these guys had no chance to be 'decent citizens.'

"I am not here to discuss their upbringing, their families, and the crack-addicted mother who was killed by the drug dealer in the living room in front of her seven-year old son. I am just trying to acknowledge that the opportunity to provide good medical care is rare anymore. I am privileged to do it now in a very unusual setting to individuals who, in general, were not the recipients of such care prior to incarceration.

"I provide care to everyone with dignity and respect and feel that is my privilege and honor. I have never been as fulfilled in my career as I am presently. It almost seems to me that my private practice had to fail or close in order to get me to my true calling: working in a maximum-security male penitentiary.

"My path started out early on at the age of five by attending Sunday school at Hawley United Methodist Church. I cannot underestimate the impact of being raised in a Christian household and the ways in which those principles played out in my daily life. I felt so strongly about my relationship with

God that I found churches to attend regularly in every place I lived, whether during college, medical school, or residency.

"My path, although circuitous at times, was always under God's loving guidance. There were several occasions that I felt as if God had forgotten about me and was challenging me in ways that I was just not capable of handling, and yet somehow I was able to continue on my journey.

"I believe all events prepare us for the upcoming road. Life may be full of challenges, heartache, pain, or suffering in order to give lessons in personal growth. I believe now in hindsight that God wanted me in prison medicine all along.

"Upon application to medical school, I was offered a public health scholarship that I declined because they could send me to work in a prison. Upon completion of my residency program, a recruiter from the federal prison provided job opportunities and again, I said, 'I am not working in a federal prison.'

"When my solo practice was failing, I was praying incessantly for direction, and one morning in church a man came up to me and said, 'Have you ever thought of working in a federal prison?' My mouth opened and I said, 'No, not ever,' but then I paused for a second and thought that perhaps God was trying to tell me something. *You have been praying for over a year about options, a man comes up to you in church and again, offers prison work—I think you should investigate it this time.*

"I am not saying I was predestined to work in the prison system. My belief is that there was a path that took many turns, but the path was somehow always trying to lead me to a job in corrections medicine.

"I have no regrets with regard to my life and the choices I have made. I believe I can appreciate things more now than perhaps I could have if I entered corrections medicine all those years ago.

"With my feet planted firmly in my faith, challenges in my life fortunately did not derail me. My personality has resulted from such life circumstances, and I feel I have weathered the storm. I have never felt alone in my pursuit of service, and I hope someday when I meet my Maker he will say, 'Job well done.'"

There is no need for the author to add commentary to Dr. Mowatt's story. Her choices were clear, and her values illuminate everything she does.

RELATIONSHIPS AND MARRIAGE

*When we long for life without difficulties,
remind us that oaks grow strong in contrary
winds and diamonds are made under pressure.*
PETER MARSHALL

MARRIAGE HAS BEEN an institution of our society for eons. Our parents were married. Our grandparents were married (usually anyway). It goes back a long, long way and always part of a family lineage. It today's society, however, people are waiting longer to get married. The average age of first marriages in the United States is now twenty-eight. Men are twenty-nine years old and women are twenty-seven. Why? Some are just not in a hurry to get married. Others wait for educational or financial reasons. And some simply don't want to get married at all.

Our society has changed quite a bit over the past fifty years. Up until the 1960s, most people got married right out of high school, usually by the time they were nineteen or twenty. Sometimes the men went off to the factories or joined the military. In most cases the women stayed home, became homemakers, and raised the children. As the sexual revolution of the 1960s progressed and women became more evident in the workplace, getting married was delayed. Now almost every family is a two-income household, because that is what it takes to have any kind of reasonable lifestyle. And because of that, finances play a big part in marriage. One of the leading causes of divorces today is money—misunderstandings, miscommunications, and completely different styles of money management. Usually when a spender and a saver get married, there are going to be problems.

There are many reasons why people get married. Some want security. Some want safety. Some feel they have found their soulmate. In other cases, it is simply a tradition and they have been raised with the belief that people are supposed get married. So why are so many people waiting longer to get married? The top reasons are either financial or educational. Marriage before or during college has declined. Only a few decades ago, high school sweethearts would marry and either went through college together or one would support the other in pursuit of their degree.

We can agree on one thing: Marriage is one of the biggest decisions people will ever make. And because it is such a big decision and supposed to be a once in a lifetime decision, they want to get it right.

Jim Rohn has a wonderful quote: "Don't wish it were easier. Wish you were better." Marriage can make you a better person because you and your spouse become two halves of a whole. It's not that the other person completes you. It's just that the two of you together can be a better couple together.

So, how do you know if marriage is the right choice for you? By definition, marriage is two people coming together to form a union. There are biblical teachings that marriage is becoming one and raising a family together. Today, though, there is a whole new context of what is considered marriage. Is a true marriage only between a man and a woman, or is a same-sex union considered marriage too? Until recently, common beliefs recognized marriage only between one man and one woman. But in 2015 the Supreme Court ruled that states cannot ban same-sex marriage. There remain arguments on both sides of the issue, both spiritual and legal. Only you can make the choice that is right for you. We believe that people get married because they find someone they really want to spend their life with.

Clearly, religious beliefs come into play in this debate. If your religious affiliation denounces same-sex marriage, then it's likely you might too. However, is it appropriate for you to impose your beliefs and values on others who may not share the same views?

Reflections by Alan:

I have discussed marriage with my two boys as they have gotten older and started dating. I've given them advice based on my own long-term marriage. I've presently been married over thirty-two years, and so far I think we've had a good marriage. We've had our ups and downs, like everyone who has been married for any extended period. There have been times where we have both wanted to walk away, but that is normal for most couples. With any kind of long-term relationship, married or not, if you love each other, there are going to be days when you can't get enough of each other and other days when you can't stand each other. You should be aware of what it takes for a marriage to work. It is not all milk and honey and happily ever after. Those situations only exist in fairy tales.

When I told my dad I wanted to get married, he said to me, "Well, you're old enough now. You have your education. You have a good job and are established now."

Then he said, "Yeah, you're ready to do this, but I'm going to give you two pieces of advice. First, don't have any kids for at least two years. The reason is that you have to get used to each other while living together. It's going to be difficult because it's much different than dating. While you may love this person, you may be crazy about this person, you may be madly in love with her, when you're living with her, things change. You must learn to accept that and work through the changes together. The reason not to have kids right away is to make sure the marriage is going to work."

My dad did not like divorce at all and he did not recommend it, but he said, "If the relationship is just not going to work, then get out of it. It is a whole lot easier to walk away when kids are not involved. Please hold off from having kids early in the marriage so you can make sure the relationship is going to stick." That alone was sage and meaningful advice.

But the second thing he told me was this, which is an old country saying: "I'm breaking your plate."

I didn't understand, so I asked him what that meant. He smiled and answered, "Well, when you move out, you're not coming back."

Now truthfully, I had no plans to come back. I figured that when I moved out and got married, I was on my own. I was going to make my way. I had no plans to go back home. What he meant was that I was leaving the nest and needed to make my own way in life from now on. In reality, I knew that if worse came to worse, my parents would be there for me (and they have been), but because Dad was direct about this, I knew I had to step up and make my own life. Some parents might want to consider that wisdom for their thirty-year-old college graduates still living in their basement.

One of the misconceptions that has been handed down from generation to generation, from our parents as well as society and our religious organizations, has led young people to believe, "You meet the love of your life when you're eighteen or twenty, and you date for a couple years. You get married and live happily ever after." That is nowhere even close to being true. Marriage is a marathon; it's not a sprint. When you are young, you want everything fast. You want it now, now, now. Even grown adults want everything immediately in this microwave society that we live in today.

The truth is that marriage *is* a long-term commitment—so choose wisely! You are agreeing to stick together through thick and thin—and there *will* be thick and thin! But in addition to commitment, a successful marriage is about compromise. Choices that you previously made on your own you will now make together. You will not always agree, but if both of you are willing to listen to each other and talk through important decisions, compromise becomes a natural state of being. You are not giving up your beliefs, wishes, or desires. You are simply approaching each choice as a priority—yours alone versus your partner's—and the key is to find the middle ground, or in many cases surrender your position because, in the grander scheme of things, it's not really that important. Typical areas of conflict include what food to eat, what movies to watch, where to go on vacation, how to spend money, and how many hours to watch football.

If you don't agree, then ask someone who has lost a long-time spouse what meant the most over the course of their marriage. You will never hear, "She would never agree to go out for Chinese food."

The obvious conclusion here is that if you expect to get your way on all decisions, you may not be the best candidate for marriage.

Reflections by Carol:

My view on marriage is based on the principles of partnership. My husband and I are closing in on thirty years together, twenty-three of them married. When we met, we were both coming out of long-term relationships, and for that reason we took things slowly. We dated, then lived together, and when the time was right, we got married. To be fair, our situation was simpler than for many other couples because children were not involved. We decided early on that we were not going to have children. We got married because we knew we wanted to spend the rest of our lives together.

But children were only one topic of discussion that formed our partnership. We learned each other's likes and dislikes; we shared the same philosophy about money; we had many interests in common and showed interest in those things that the other was passionate about. I can remember the first time he introduced me to his project car. It was a 1962 Chevy Impala convertible. To say that it was a "car" is being generous; all I saw was a rusted body on blocks. He saw the vision of what it would look like after a total restoration. He saw an investment; I saw a money pit. He saw hours of enjoyment; I saw hours of being a garage widow.

I made a choice to not treat the car as my competition or my enemy. I learned to love it by seeing it through his eyes. That car became a symbol of our relationship. And it was a two-way street. One of my passions is crafting—specifically dried flower arrangements and Christmas decorations. Every time I would come home with packages from Michael's or JoAnn's or A. C. Moore, my husband would cringe a little, and I would smile and say something like, "How's that new tool you bought last week working out?"

By exploring those things you have in common as well as those you don't share, you begin to carve out space in the relationship. You need space for yourself; your partner needs space; and you need space together. This is a key component of any relationship, but it's essential in a long-term relationship. Give each other the elbowroom to grow. Think of two vines planted side by side at the base of a trellis. Each needs water, fertilizer, and sunlight to grow. As they climb the trellis, they stretch to intertwine their leaves, creating a beautiful, full, and natural shape. The viewer only sees the combined effect, but at the base of each vine, each is still nourished by water, fertilizer, and sunlight. If those elements are cut off from either vine, they will die.

The principles of partnership in a successful business include equality, transparency, being results-oriented, responsibility, and complementary skills. Think about your own relationship. Do you treat each other as equals? Are you completely honest with each other? Do you share the same goals? Does each partner take responsibility for their role (simple things like taking out the garbage, walking the dog, making the bed, or paying the bills)? And do you bring different strengths to the table that complement each other?

If you can answer yes to those questions, chances are you have a solid relationship. If you hesitated on any of the questions, then look for ways to improve.

Like all business partnerships, you may have to renegotiate the terms of your marriage from time to time. But how long do you wait to address an issue? Do you ignore it and hope it will solve itself? Perhaps this will help: There is a difference between a "flare up" and a "meltdown." Think of the difference between a brush fire and a raging inferno. Brush fires can be contained and tamped out quickly if you are paying attention. Raging infernos are difficult to contain and often lead to total destruction.

Marriages work the same way. When you have a "flare up," make the choice to deal with it immediately. Power through those difficult conversations. It's not that hard if you focus on two things: 1) talk only about the issue that's upsetting you today—avoid bringing up every other thing that bugs you, and 2) don't make it personal; preserve your partner's dignity and replace "what's wrong" with "what's right."

Meltdowns mean you have let things go too far and too long without addressing them. What started out as an annoyance becomes an obsession, and that could lead you down the path to divorce. Don't wait for the meltdown when something isn't going right.

But even when you spot a flare-up, take a moment to assess whether it is really a potential problem, or just something affecting you badly on that particular day. Be honest with yourself first. What the other person is doing or saying may be viewed through a clouded lens. Perhaps the real problem is elsewhere—something totally unrelated—and our partner's action becomes the flash point for our wrath. In other words, "don't kick the dog." It won't do anything to preserve or enhance his loyalty or trust in you.

The bottom line is that marriage is more about commitment and compromise than being madly in love. It begins long before you reach the altar. When you are in love and before you get married, it's easy to look past the things that might drive a wedge between you over time. We're not talking about annoying habits like leaving the toilet seat up, not replacing the cap on the toothpaste, or failing to fill the car with gas. The more serious flaws somehow become amplified when rings are exchanged. You want to change the things you don't like in your partner. Banish that idea from your mind. You cannot and should not try to change another human being. The sooner you make a choice to accept them as they are (the person they were *before* you married them), the more likely your marriage will last.

Do not interpret this as cynical thinking. There is no question that love is the glue that holds the marriage together, but if you add "like" and "accept" to that feeling called "love," you are on your way to years of happiness. It's all in your attitude and your approach.

This brings us to another important aspect of commitment and compromise. One that is often overlooked or ignored before marriage, and that's the *family* you are marrying. They are not taking the same vows as you and your spouse. But regardless of his or her relationship with family and despite your feelings about family in-law members, they are part of what you signed on for. Finding the strength to extend your energies around commitment and compromise to include them will minimize stress and add years of peace and maybe even harmony to your marriage. It's your choice.

There is no magic formula to know if your marriage is going to work. Only time will tell. This may be why so many young adults are delaying marriage in favor of cohabitation. Some justify moving in together because they're sleeping together anyway. It is almost always more economical, and it is probably more convenient. Putting any moral argument aside, it is a practical solution and a way to take the relationship for a "test drive."

As the saying goes, "you don't really know a person until you've lived with them." This is true, but research on the subject of cohabitation confirms that when you live together, you are not *committed* fully to the relationship, and you are less willing to *compromise*. What you are learning about your mate is only what they want you to see, and either of you can walk away at any time. There are those words again: commitment and compromise.

We are not advocating for nor campaigning against marriage or cohabitation, nor are we condemning shotgun marriages or quickie divorces. The challenge is to dig deep and make the choice that's right for you. Whether you live together or choose to get married, you and your chosen partner both deserve a 100 percent investment in each other and the partnership.

Our next story is about a girl who spent much of her life rejecting relationships. Her journey is testimony to the pain and loneliness so many of us experience when we can't connect in a meaningful way with another human being.

She was only four years old when she first rejected love. Louise was a precocious child, and one day in her kindergarten class during a game of Farmer in the Dell, a little boy picked her out of the group and declared he wanted her to be his wife. Louise cried and screamed and ran from the class yelling, "I don't want to be anyone's wife!"

Even at this tender age, the emotional scars were deep. She was growing up in a family that wasn't safe. One night, hiding behind a door, she watched while her dad knocked out her mother's teeth. Another time she cowered at the top of the stairs when the police crashed through the front door with shotguns drawn. A neighbor had reported another fight.

Louise had no concept of a healthy relationship. The pattern was reinforced when her mom began abusing Louise and her sibling. Her life at home was about fear and danger, and those feelings were tied to family relationships. At a gut, visceral level, she wasn't willing to do that anymore.

She started developing early and was attractive to boys, but she always treated them badly, always pushing them away. At seventeen, her desire for sex was strong, but only in circumstances where she was in control. She became promiscuous and sought value and self-worth through the act of sex without intimacy. She wouldn't let anyone get close. She found married men to be the solution to keeping her walls up because they couldn't put demands on her time or her heart.

There were attempts at relationships during her early twenties. In fact, she got engaged three times. She loved the parties and the jewelry, and it kept people from questioning her. However, when thing got too close, she always found a way to sabotage and ruin the relationship.

Turning inward as a defense mechanism is not an uncommon thing for people to do, but it doesn't solve the problem. Louise was lost, and there didn't seem to be a way out from the pattern of destructive behavior.

At twenty-five she met the man she would eventually marry. However, it did not take long for the same old patterns to emerge. One of her friends asked her why didn't feel she deserved to be happy. Louise answered, "Because I can't count on anyone. I couldn't count on my parents. And he will fail me too."

It was the first time Louise came face-to-face with her feelings. She made a choice that day to change. She didn't exactly know how she was going to do it, and she didn't even know *what* to do, but the drama in her story stems from a simple mental switch.

Over the next three years, the relationship with her future husband had its ups and downs, its periods of off and on, but something kept them together. Ironically, they had similar backgrounds, and therefore they decided therapy would help both of them. The first year was rough. One night he found Louise in the corner of their closet, hiding behind the clothes, cowering in fear. There had been no violence; they merely had a disagreement over something inconsequential.

Gently taking her into his arms, he said, "My goal is for you to feel safe. You don't have to fight to get what you need." When he kissed her on the cheek, for the first time she felt a sense of peace. She knew it was going to be OK and she would spend the rest of her life with him.

Even though she had made her choice to change several years before, the true learning started from that point and became a seven-year process for Louise. In her case, making a choice was only a step in a new direction. It was not a life-changing moment; bells didn't ring, and the world did not suddenly become a brighter place. This is the most important lesson of her story.

Life is a process, and sometimes the choice we make is simply to alter our course. But to think things will magically change and the past will melt away is naïve.

"You have to learn how to let people in and be vulnerable. I am proud of how far I've come, and I'm an example that deep healing is possible. I wouldn't have gotten this far without my husband."

That last point is profound because the person who rejected everyone and was so closed inwardly started out believing she could change on her own. It was only through opening herself up and accepting the love of another person that her course changed.

When asked where she is now and what advice she has for others, this is what she said: "I tell people I love them—because I do. The love is in my heart. But I am not the first person to hug. I need my three feet of personal space. I do believe that people need people. It is a combination of behavioral, biological, biochemical, even quantum physics. Every day I step through the fear of trusting others. But I now believe that there are very few people who set out to do harm. I no longer hold grudges, and I don't hold hatred in my heart."

One of the most enlightened points she made was her own acceptance of the fact that people are going to fail you. How you deal with it is what makes the difference. "I focus now on doing better for me and the people around me. I was incapable of doing that before. My only regret is the harm and hurt I have caused others.

"When I do screw up, I don't waste time judging or second guessing myself. I just say, 'next time' and move forward. Dwelling on the past is where I lived for too many years."

One of the challenges she puts to herself and others is to not compromise, but instead learn to express yourself differently, not destructively. Sometimes it can be as simple as saying, "This is not acceptable to me."

She now inspires and guides others through her writing, speaking, and coaching. "I tell someone who is struggling to be ready to walk away from relationships that don't serve them. Healthy boundaries are the foundation for relationships. People don't know your boundaries if you don't tell them, and having uncomfortable conversations is required.

"My mantra is that 'no' is a whole and compete sentence. Most people don't get that, and you will probably have to explain it. While you don't owe people an explanation when you say no, sometimes they deserve it. People want to understand you, and more of them are on your side than not. This was the hardest lesson for me to learn."

Louise and her husband are coming up on their twenty-fifth anniversary. She shared that working on their communication with each other is the most important skill they've mastered. "It didn't come easy for us because we both came to the relationship with baggage, but it was worth the effort. Like many marriages, we went through a few rough patches, but we made it through because of the foundation we built years before."

For someone who spent many years rejecting human connection, it has become has her strongest value. The very thing she rallied against is now what drives her. She refers to it as honoring the Namaste—the light in you! She finally found it with her parents. Before her father died, they had long conversations. He took responsibility for his actions, and she, in turn, took responsibility for everything that happened after she turned eighteen. "Mom is still working on her stuff, so our relationship is more guarded. I understand her, but I have set strict boundaries. I need to be in a healthy space, and she still cannot give that to me. But we keep working at it."

Another value she holds dearly is self-love, which includes self-worth. "I am going to love me most . . . and not apologize for that." She teaches people how to treat her and believes that if you don't love yourself first, why would you expect anyone else to love you?

Louise is no longer a victim, and she has stopped being a victimizer. Breaking patterns of destructive behavior is without a doubt a very difficult thing to do. She encourages anyone in a situation of substance abuse or addiction issues (including sex, money, gambling, drugs, or alcohol) to realize that bad behaviors are not learned in a vacuum. When you are drowning, you don't have a complete grasp or control on reality. You lose sight of the goodness of life. Growth stops when abuse comes into play. You will start growing again when you break those chains and alter those patterns.

For Ginger, the problem was different. She had no problem allowing men in her life. She wanted to be married, but it took years for her to break a pattern of making the same wrong choice over and over again.

Ginger was born in Quebec, Canada, but raised in New England. As a teenager, she had low self-esteem; she was skinny and flat-chested; she was the girl everyone looked past. It was only with her family that she had a place. She had a loving family, but her father and brothers always came first. She grew up watching her mother tend to their every need.

She adored her father and, like many young girls, always strove to please him. All the while she struggled with believing in herself. As she grew, so did her body. This gorgeous, voluptuous redhead caught the eye of every man she met. The more attention they gave her, the more she morphed into what they expected. The more exaggerated her behavior became, the more her self-esteem plummeted.

"I believed I wasn't that good of a person, but if I could help somebody else, I would become a better person." Unfortunately, that somewhat misguided belief caused her to gravitate to men who weren't good for her. Men who, she learned too late, had their own mental health problems.

Husband number one was broken. He was one of fourteen kids, and his father committed suicide when he was four years old. His mom died when he was nine. He was bounced around until high school when he was taken in by an aunt along with his triplet sisters. When he met Ginger, he was attracted to her family life, but at the same time he was jealous of her relationship with her family. It wasn't long before he became physically abusive.

The pattern was a familiar one: The abuse wasn't constant, incidents were always followed with lots of remorse, and she didn't realize she could just walk out. She believed she needed his permission to leave, and he wouldn't agree to a divorce.

This went on for two and a half years, chipping away at her dignity and her soul. Her husband was an athletic type, and one day when he was preparing to leave for a game, he flew into a rage because she hadn't washed his jockstrap. Something snapped in her that day. "I knew I deserved better than this. I was going to leave no matter what, but this time he agreed to the divorce. It wasn't until afterward that I learned he had found a mistress."

Ginger waited seven years until she married again. She was now thirty-two years old and had been dating this man for only a few months. He proposed in front of his class at school and she was too scared to say no because she didn't want to hurt his feelings. She knew immediately it wasn't the right decision. He adored her, but she didn't love him. This time she suffered emotional abuse. He knew she didn't really love him and tortured her with guilt and humiliation. The marriage lasted only one year, and then she walked out on him. He was married to someone else two months later.

I asked her which was worse for her, the physical abuse or the emotional abuse. "There is no worse. With the physical you're scared. And with the emotional you're beaten down." She could walk away but not without deepening the scars that already existed.

It was on the rebound that she met husband number three. He was charming and persuasive; he showered her with flowers and gifts. He made her feel like she was special. They were married after nine months. This time the marriage lasted less nine months. On their wedding night, everything changed. "You're my wife now, and you'll do what I tell you." This Dr. Jeckle and Mr. Hyde came out of nowhere. Had she missed the signs? Had he tricked her?

She knew now she had choices, but they were trampled when the beating began. He was even more abusive than husband number one. He would beat on her for hours but never touched her face. The cruelty of his open fist combined with his version of mental abuse, "You are on your third marriage; *you* are the problem." For reasons she never fully understood, he did agree to counseling, but he never really changed.

One night he came home drunk at one in the morning and woke her up. "I knew at that moment he could have killed me. In his drunken condition, he was just vulnerable enough to give me my opening. I pushed him on the couch and ran with only my keys in my hands. I went to a girlfriend's house."

"He showed up a week later, but my friend wouldn't let him see me. After that I knew I had to get farther away, so I went home to my family. I felt helpless, stupid, and alone. I was broken. As fate would have it, I called our phone number when I knew he wouldn't be home to check for messages. There was a message from his mistress declaring her undying love for him. That was my leverage to get the divorce."

After that, Ginger went through a total change. She stayed with her family and used that time to reflect. For the first time she asked herself, "Why are you making these choices?" She realized that in following this pattern of seeking to help others and make them feel better about themselves, she had lost herself. It was then that she made the choice: "From now on I come first!"

Her message to all the women out there is, "When anyone comes to you with a sob story . . . run for the hills."

The wonderful thing about Ginger's story is that she did find herself and she also found her true soul mate. When she met her fourth husband, she knew immediately he wasn't needy at all. He was honest, hardworking, and enjoyed time with her family. They met when he was on a hunting trip with her father. There were no underlying motives; he was a straight shooter. There was no manipulation. She had learned to read the signs and ask the right questions. "The most important thing I knew was that he wasn't jealous or possessive, a characteristic that all three of my former husbands shared. I had complete trust."

Ginger's story is about making bad choices over and over, repeating a cycle of destruction. It wasn't until she escaped to a safe place and took the time reflect that she was able to gain the confidence and the wisdom to make better choices.

Ginger's advice to anyone in a bad situation is to listen to your friends. "When friends say, 'You're a completely different person when you're with him,' it's a huge red flag. You are not being true to yourself."

Love, honesty, and trust must be there for a relationship to work. "I never looked for those things, because I thought they should be automatic. And if they weren't there at the beginning, I could fix it—I could make it so.

"When I spent that time with my family after failed marriage number three, one of my closest friends said to me, "What is going on with you? You are the one making these choices . . . no one else." That was when Ginger realized that she was indeed in control.

"It helps to have support. For me, it was my friends and my family—they were huge. My father was my hero. He was appalled when he learned what I had gone through. I never told them. In fact, I never spoke about my relationships when I was in the relationship."

It was only afterward that she could talk about them. By her own admission, it was a mistake to keep quiet. "There are so many places I could have gone for help, but I didn't. No one should suffer in silence."

She met her current husband at age thirty-seven, and they lived together for eighteen months before they got married. Ginger laid down the rules right away. There was no gray area this time about what she wanted and what she expected.

Her advice is to know what you need and be clear about what is acceptable to you. If you know it's not OK, don't let it build up. It will only get worse. It's up to each person to make their own rules and then find the right person—someone who will treat them the way they should be treated.

When we discussed values, she admitted that her values were always there, but they were clouded by her own insecurities to live up to them. "Today I can say with certainly that I value myself as a person. I am so fortunate to be who I am and love myself. I still have an innate desire to help others, but I'm better equipped to do it now."

She said that if she could have a conversation with her younger self, she would tell her, "Value yourself. Don't let anybody make you feel like shit about yourself."

How do relationships and values intersect, and does it matter? This can be everything from friends to relationships with neighbors, colleagues at work, and spousal/partnership relationships. Do we gravitate to or repel people because we don't share the same value systems? And how do we know? Sometimes we don't know up front what someone's values are, and it's not until they are tested or they reveal their true self that the relationship goes deeper or breaks apart and disintegrates.

Think of a time in a relationship (it doesn't matter what kind) when suddenly it was as though a lightbulb went off and you saw that person with absolute clarity for the first time. What happened? What triggered it? What shifted? What did they show? How did they show it? And what did it mean to you? Did it cause you to have a deeper appreciation for this person, a true understanding of what they stood for, or was it the opposite? Did you suddenly see this person for who they truly were, and it wasn't very pretty? It conflicted with your values and caused you to question anything they had ever said and done prior to that moment. How did you handle it? This is the real test. How do you handle those revelations?

When your boss makes a decision that you truly didn't expect, what are the consequences to you, the company, the organization, the customers, the other employees? There are many people who know that their core values conflict with the companies they work for, but sometimes there are reasons they must stay in those jobs. Maybe there's a scarcity of jobs in the area. Maybe they don't feel they have the skills to market themselves and go elsewhere. Maybe they're being paid so well and it's like buying their conscience—they can turn the other cheek, look the other way—they can accept the fact that the company compromises their values because that's not them. They are just doing their job and taking a paycheck. Wow! Here's a big question. How are you not compromising your own values by taking money from the people who are fundamentally doing things that you think are wrong?

Whistle-blowers would fall into the category of those who stand up for what's right. Knowing full well that the consequences may be dire, they risk losing their job, their friends, and their position; they might get blacklisted and not be employable elsewhere. But it is so important to them to do what they think is right that they have to let the world know.

One of the reasons there is so much debate around Michael Snowden is this very issue. Those who advocate and support what he did feel the information he put out there was something the American public was entitled to know and it was being hidden from them. Those who don't support him see his actions as treason that put the whole country in a compromising situation because of the sensitivity of the information. Whether you agree or disagree with Snowden's actions, you must acknowledge the fact his actions were driven by his core values. The only question is whether they were misguided or executed improperly, and that's probably the middle-ground debate. Could he have accomplished the same thing but done it differently?

That debate will rage on for generations. What matters is how important your values are to you and what choices you make when they are put to the test in any relationship, personal or business. Are your values elastic? Do they stretch to adapt to the circumstances? Do you compromise your values in favor of someone or something else? Or are your values clear to you and to the important relationships in your life?

SCARCITY VERSUS ABUNDANCE

*Happiness is not something ready-made.
It comes from your own actions.*
Dalai Lama

IF YOU ARE among the middle class, it is no surprise to you there is an economic inequality in the United States. While statistics vary depending on the source, you can be assured that the richest 1 percent hold about 38 percent of all privately held wealth, while the bottom 90 percent hold 73 percent of the debt. The four hundred richest Americans now have more wealth than the bottom 61 percent of the entire population.

Some liberal thinkers believe that wealth should be redistributed equally to reset the scales and give everyone an equal footing. But studies suggest that if you took all the money in the world and divided it equally among every single person on the planet, within ten years the money would flow back roughly to where it is today. Why is that true? The reason is quite simple really.

When someone grows up poor, living paycheck to paycheck, and they have limited skills when it comes to budgeting, buying, and borrowing, they are not equipped to handle money. Contributing factors are limited education, drug or alcohol abuse, criminal records, few job skills, or mental health issues. The mere concept of leveraging money for long-term stability and security seems foreign and unattainable. What happens in most cases when there is an influx of unexpected gain (such as winning the lottery), within a short period of time, the money is gone.

At the opposite end of the spectrum are those who grew up with means. Often the super-rich families are wealthy with assets that have accumulated over generations. There is an inherent attitude about money—how to get it, grow it, and keep it. If wealth is lost, they possess the belief and skills to rebuild. As you would expect, the contributing factors are education, career skills, and a strong network of other highly successful people.

There is an obvious dichotomy here that's worth pointing out. If you are surrounded by impoverished, underprivileged, and uneducated people, you are at an extreme disadvantage to change your mind-set and your circumstances. It can be done—and it *is* done—but it is not easy. If, on the other hand, you are surrounded by the comforts of wealth and people who understand and appreciate how to leverage or invest money to make it grow, you have a huge advantage in sustaining that lifestyle.

So what is behind this chasm in our society? And what can you do to change your circumstances if you are not among the uber-wealthy but would like to improve your financial footing? Believe it or not, it doesn't start with education or finding new friends. It starts with your attitude.

The concepts of scarcity versus abundance has been widely researched, and the patterns are undeniable. Two of our favorite thought leaders who have written volumes on the subject are John Maxwell and Stephen Covey.

Covey says:

> People with a scarcity mentality tend to see everything in terms of win-lose. There is only so much; and if someone else has it, that means there will be less for me. The more principle-centered we become, the more we develop an abundance mentality, the more we are genuinely happy for the successes, well-being, achievements, recognition, and good fortune of other people. We believe their success adds to . . . rather than detracts from . . . our lives.

John Maxwell offers:

> Sometimes we hold on to our possessions because we fear we might run out—life seems scarce. But when we believe that giving is the way to live, we will produce more in the future—life seems abundant.

It seems pretty simple. If you hold onto things, they can't grow. If you give them away, they will expand and flourish. We are both old enough to remember what it was like to go to the bank with our passbook savings and add a few dollars to our account every month. The excitement of seeing the teller stamp that book and tell you your account earned an extra $1.25 last month made you giddy. It was money you didn't earn by doing anything other than putting it in the bank. But if that money had been put under the mattress, it would have stayed stagnant with no hope of becoming any more valuable than it was when you put it there.

That's a good metaphor for how to begin to change your life. What assets are you holding onto that could grow if you only shared them? And this isn't limited to money. What experience do you have that you can share with others? What life lessons, good or bad, could benefit someone younger or needier than you? How can you change your routine to include new and different people in your life? What can you learn from them? How will you both benefit? Jim Rohn calls this "creating something from nothing." An artist has vision in his or her mind and then creates that vision through painting or another art form. This book was created by the thoughts of Carol and Alan.

Abundant thinking is expansive thinking. It is lifting your head and looking outward. The world is full of possibilities if you only take time to look for them. We have discussed in other chapters the impact of technology, the deluge of information that blasts us every day, and the stress of our workaday lives. The bad news is that this is not going to change. The good news is that this is not going to change. The challenge in front of every one of us is learning how to seize it as an opportunity rather than a crushing burden.

If you are a fan of social media, you know it is a fabulous way to stay connected. But have you moved past your friends and family network on Facebook? Do you have a LinkedIn profile, and if you do, when was the last time you looked at it? Does your profile reflect the power of who you are and position you for what you want to become? Are you connected to a network of influencers who can open doors for you to meet new people or secure new options? LinkedIn is firmly positioned in the social media world as the "professional networking site," but you don't have to be a high-ranking executive or self-employed professional to benefit. There is not a person, including you, who doesn't have a teacher, a friend, a neighbor, or a colleague that doesn't know at least a dozen other people who could aid you in getting from where you are to where you want to be.

Here's another challenge. Every day you do something. You go to work. You volunteer. You attend church. You play sports. Typically, conversations in any of those settings remain focused on what you are there to do. Believe it or not, if you narrow yourself to those limitations, that is an example of scarcity thinking. Conversely, if you seek ways to talk to individuals with you about anything other than the subject of what brought you together, amazing things can happen.

Go beyond the idle and usually meaningless banter. "How was traffic?" "What do you think of this weather we're having?" "How are you today?" That's a start, but consider it only the icebreaker. Ask just one person if they would like to sit and chat. Start with, "It occurred to me that I only know you as Tiffany's mother. I would like to know a little about you. Tell me about yourself." Or you can try, "I heard you were interested in music. I never knew that about you. How did it start?"

The doors to abundant thinking need only to be cracked open. There is no single magic formula that will change your life overnight. The secret is to keep exploring. Look for new answers to your questions, new solutions to your problems; open your mind and heart to people who are not like you and really listen to what they say—and by all means, start reading. We have provided a list of recommended resources at the end of the book.

Reflections by Alan:

I'd like to approach this topic from a slightly different angle. Let's talk about motivation. My question is, "Should someone who doesn't want to work make the same amount of money as someone who went to school, earned a degree, learned a trade, and puts in twelve or thirteen hours a day? Should they make the same amount of money as someone who stays at home and does nothing all day?"

That depends! If a person sits at home and does "nothing" all day but comes up with an invention that will help the world, then OK, that's fine. But if they're just staying home and watching TV all day, should they make the same amount of money? Most people would say no. Let's look at that.

One person goes out and works eight, ten, twelve, fourteen, or sixteen hours a day; another person stays home and watches TV. Who should earn more, who should make more, who should be rewarded? Realistically it should be the person who did more work. Right? There's a verse in the Bible that says, "For even when we were with you, we gave you this rule: 'The one who is unwilling to work shall not eat.'" (2 Thessalonians 3:10, NIV).

For people who are ill, in bad health, or disabled, it's an entirely different story, but in general, I believe that someone who is able-bodied and capable should go out and work, if there's work available.

For that person who is a sloth, why do they choose scarcity or not doing very much over the possibility of having more? A lot of it, I believe, has to do with fear, especially the fear of failing. They are afraid that if they go out and actually try to accomplish something, they might fail or they might be embarrassed, so why try? They decide to just do the minimum and live on what they have. They don't want to put in any more effort than necessary. They are good with what they have, which is just enough.

In some cases, their belief system may instill the idea that abundance, from a monetary standpoint, is a sin. Some believe that being poor makes you humble and more worthy in the eyes of God. They do not focus on money or material possessions; they just survive on what they have and they are happy with that. If that's the case, people like this are not the best candidates for change.

On the other hand, some people have a fear of succeeding. I love one of Thomas Edison's quotes: "If we did all the things we are capable of, we would literally astound ourselves." For some, that is simply overwhelming.

I believe that many people are afraid of succeeding because if they do succeed, their friends may not like them anymore because they've gotten ahead of them. Our friend Glenn Morshower calls this "outshining"—meaning that your friends and family want you to shine, but not outshine them. Many cultures around the world feel you should be humble and thankful for what you have and not try to do better. As humans, we naturally value being involved, being part of a group, and being accepted. It takes internal drive and confidence to step out of the circle and make choices that will move us forward.

But what if you are young and ill-equipped to handle the concept of scarcity and abundance? What if someone in your family has caused your world to collapse? This brings us to the story of Megan.

"Dad worked on Wall Street and was convicted for something he didn't do. When the bank went under, he testified against them, but in the end, he and two others went to prison. I was fourteen years old, and my privileged life evaporated."

That's where Megan's story begins. How does a young teenager survive when her family is in the headlines of an international story for crimes she doesn't fully understand and the father she knows and loves is now a pariah of society?

Her family sent her away at fifteen as an exchange student, hoping that by the time she returned home, the publicity would have died down and things would have returned to normal. No one thought her father would be convicted, but he was, and when she returned as a junior in high school, she was the outsider. Her class wasn't sympathetic.

Megan's story is being told by a mature, successful woman in her mid-fifties. "When I was an exchange student at the age of fifteen, I spoke to an audience of 1,500 people, and I've been speaking ever since—but only recently have I found my voice."

That vulnerable and embarrassed child of fifteen started making bad choices. She was surrounded by a mother who took up drinking and a father who took up the sport when he got out of prison. The lives they knew had been shattered, and everyone was struggling to regain balance.

Her mom never wanted to talk about what happened. Friends who she thought were friends abandoned her. Money became the ugly betrayer in the house; there was never enough, and the message Megan heard was scarcity. She was on her own.

"I never stood up for myself when I should have. Learning to stand up for yourself is the choice I didn't make. It has taken me a long time."

Megan's story is one of struggle, mistakes, and regrets, yet also tenacity. The story she shared is one that many can relate to. When you are in a situation beyond your control, it is easy to lose yourself and begin to act out. It becomes your own form of control, but it seldom produces positive results.

Megan's life has been a roller coaster of big successes and many bumps along the way. Marriage, children, divorce, a wounded relationship with an alcoholic mother, and damaged self-esteem.

Despite all that, Megan got her college degree and has been a successful entrepreneur for over twenty years. She has dealt with the scars of her youth and has raised troubled teens on her own. Her business has flourished and languished depending the economic tides, but her survival instincts have always given her the fuel to power through.

Megan attracted friends who did not appreciate her and fell into negative patterns and self-doubt. But her story offers hope and inspiration to anyone living an unsettled or unresolved life.

Megan has declared this to be her "Fuck You Fifties." One of the deliberate and conscious choices she made recently was to move farther away from her mother, her ex-husband, and her defective friendships. "I now stand up for myself more quickly. I decided I wasn't going to put up with bullshit anymore. I'm speaking out more; doing what I should have done a decade earlier (it should have been the Fuck You Forties!)."

What can you learn from Megan's story? She says that daring yourself to take risks and not be held back by other small-minded people is where it all starts. Don't surround yourself with others who are needier than you; it only drags you down. Don't stay in the box and say, "woe is me." Keep reaching for the stars.

Start by acknowledging that the good you already have in your life (and everybody has some good) is the foundation for all abundance.

Megan says, "I learned not to focus on the *why*. Why don't I have more money? Why is my business sagging? Why don't my kids appreciate what I'm doing for them?" This negative thinking only makes things worse.

Instead, Megan's advice is to reframe those questions. "What can I do to make more money? What actions can I take today to secure one new client? What can I do to make my kids feel good about themselves?" When you focus on forward movement, movement happens.

Just in making the choice to shed the paradigm of her past has propelled Megan forward. And there is little doubt that changing her environment was a big part of that. Not everyone can pick up and move—or can they? Limiting beliefs will always hold you back, and until you step up and punch them squarely in the face, you won't know the true limits of your capability.

Megan is a perfect example of someone whose values have protected her every step of the way. They were always there, but she unwittingly suppressed them because of her own insecurities, self-doubt, and fear. That fragile, hurt child had all the tools she needed all along, but she failed to access them.

She believes that every single human being has the capacity to tap into that inner self and break free of attitudes and limitations that have been holding them back.

Let's look at the values that kept Megan going and are now just fully blossoming. They include honesty, relationships, creativity, sense of being, love, and appreciation. By turning them loose in the universe instead of holding them hostage, you open up a new world of possibility.

She ended our interview with a quote from Abraham. "You are the owner of all that you perceive. But you can't perceive apart from your vibration. Feel your way, little by little, into a greater sense of abundance by looking for the treasures that the Universe is offering you on a day-to-day basis."

Megan's story represents the journey from young girl to womanhood. Her ability to put one foot in front of the other and keep going illuminates the capacity that each of us possesses to deal with whatever comes our way. It may take time and patience, but it is worth taking that first step and making that first choice.

The principles of abundant thinking apply to everyone and every stage of economic status. Millionaires want to hang out with billionaires because they want to learn about what they do. How do they live their lives? How do they think? How do they operate? What businesses do they pursue? What investments do they make?

If your savings account is anemic, your 401K nonexistent, if you sacrifice eating out because you must pay the rent this month, then you may not be ready for hanging out with billionaires or even millionaires, but there is a clear path forward. If you're making minimum wage, then talk to a person in a salaried position: a medical technician, a computer programmer, a veterinary assistant, a policeman—you fill in the blank. Look at what appeals to you and find out what others did to get there. Then follow those directions. This is called modeling someone who has achieved what you want to do.

If you have a lower-level job and you want to move up, talk to your office manager, your field supervisor, or a human resource professional. Find out what steps you must take to get that promotion.

And if you're considering breaking out on your own and starting your own business, talk to other business owners or interview franchise owners in the brand you are considering. Find the closest SCORE chapter in your area. (SCORE is a nonprofit association dedicated to helping small businesses get off the ground through education and mentorship, and it's all free!)

If you want something more for your life and your family, examine your thoughts and patterns. Are you approaching life with an attitude of scarcity or abundance? There's only one choice, and it's yours for the taking.

SELF-DISCOVERY

*Do one thing every day
that scares you.*
ANONYMOUS

THE ROAD TO self-discovery is different for every one of us. When you hear a child declare that they want to be a fireman when they grow up, you smile in bemusement because you know that will change as assuredly as the summer fades to fall.

When an adult declares, "I've got to figure out what I want to be when I grow up," bemusement is replaced with curiosity or sometimes even judgment. How can a mature person not know who they are and what they want out of life? You'd be surprised how many people are grappling with that very question.

We don't make it easy for people in transition. We expect there to be a clear path; a beginning (college), a middle (your job), and an end (retirement). But those days of absolute direction have faded, and in their place we wrestle with the big questions. Who am I? Why am I here? What is my purpose? What will my legacy be? Will anybody care?

There is not a person over the age of forty who doesn't look back on a choice they made at an earlier age and ask themselves, "What was I thinking?" Sometimes this is followed up with "I wasn't thinking" and other times with "If I had it to do all over again, I would do the exact same thing."

Our first story in this chapter may seem out of place. It focuses on choices made at a time shortly after college with implications that touch on personal choice, self-discovery, beliefs, and judgment. We'll let you draw your own conclusion.

Mary's story began with a choice she made when she was just twenty-four years old. She is now in her late sixties and has had time to reflect on the impact of the series of choices she made in her life and what they mean to her now.

Mary grew up in the 1960s, a time known for its freedom of expression and a generation that challenged the status quo. Gone was the fear of voicing one's opinion that overshadowed her parents' generation, due in part to the McCarthy Era as well as a renewed focus on family and career rather than activism following World War II and Korea.

Now, Mary was not into the flower child, drug-addled, commune-type of life, but she embraced a desire to explore her identity, her sexuality, and her beliefs. She did not want to be held back by the social systems, the mores, or even necessarily the values that had grounded her as a youth. To put it in perspective, let's remember what was happening in the sixties. The flower-child generation emerged because of passion for what they perceived was wrong in the world. It was centered around the injustices of the Vietnam War. Protests were taking place on college campuses throughout the United States, and Mary was in the heart of it.

She was on a campus in Washington, D.C., where protestors came face-to-face with the seat of government; tempers on both sides of the debate were blistering, and passions were exploding. Ironically, Mary watched most of it from the sidelines. She wasn't sure what she really felt or believed. Was she against the war or for it? Did she support the veterans, or was she against the government and the establishment? She shared this as a reflection of the inner turmoil that touched all aspects of her life in her search for identity and independence.

While Mary was steadfast in her resolve never to use drugs, she had a love affair with alcohol. Barhopping and over-indulgence was the norm; along with that came the courage to be sexually indiscriminate. Sex with a variety of partners became Mary's pattern; she even kept score in her Hallmark pocket calendar. Relationships rarely lasted long, but it didn't matter because she wasn't looking for a husband like many of her classmates. She was exploring her unchartered self while pursuing her education.

"We didn't have the concerns of STDs or AIDs—yes, there was always the issue of getting pregnant, but there was birth control, and I used it most of the time. I was a virgin until I was nineteen, and once uncorked, I just went for it."

And that's the foundation of Mary's story about choice. You see, Mary did get pregnant at age twenty-four when she was in her first serious relationship.

This was the man she was going to marry, and that's where it got complicated. Her fiancé was in the process of getting a divorce and already had three children of his own. Before he met Mary, he had made a choice of his own to have a vasectomy to avoid additional trauma as his marriage was crumbling. So when Mary got pregnant, she knew he could not be the father.

She had gotten pregnant by someone she knew casually, and as it happened, they had one night of indiscretion while away at a conference. Neither had any expectations as he was married and she was in love with someone else. Mary didn't hesitate in her decision. There was no point in wrecking his life or her life, so she got an abortion without telling anyone. She never questioned her decision.

Mary was quick to point out that during this time, abortions, while not common, were not as controversial as they are today. The pro-life movement had not begun, and Roe v. Wade opened the door to an easier solution if a mistake was made. It was between the woman and her doctor, and the choice was hers.

Mary got married the next summer and was gloriously happy for some time until the marriage began to falter. The reasons are not germane to this story, but suffice it say, she and her husband were at different places in their lives, and the future was uncertain. Mary had a close friend from work and intimate conversations about her marital woes led to an extramarital affair.

She got pregnant again. This time the consequences and the stakes were much higher. Not only would it have been the final blow to her marriage, but the father was someone she cared about, and he was also married. The other relevant fact during this time was that Mary's career was beginning to soar, and having a baby was not in the cards.

She had a second abortion because she felt it was the right choice at the time for her and for those who would have been affected. It was easy . . . it was affordable . . . it was private. . . . Because of this scare, she ended the affair, recommitted to her marriage, and continued to focus on her career.

Mary wishes that was the end of her story, but there is another chapter. Ultimately her marriage did end. It wasn't dramatic; it was simply that two people had grown apart, had different goals in life, and could no longer satisfy each other's needs, so they decided to divorce. It was amicable, but it was painful, as all divorces are.

Mary shared that over the years she had learned that being in a relationship was very important to her. It wasn't long before she found someone else. The difference with this person was that he never wanted to have children.

This suited Mary because at her age and the trajectory of her career, and after one failed marriage, she didn't want children either. After years of being married to a man who couldn't have children, birth control was no longer a habit, and yes, Mary got pregnant again. This time she talked it out with her then fiancé, and together they decided that a child was not in their future, so Mary had a third abortion.

In the years when these relationships were taking place—while her career was blossoming and she was young and vibrant—those decisions, made at three different times and for three different reasons, were the right choices for Mary. They were not accidental choices; they were conscious choices based on the information she had in front of her and the circumstances she faced.

But now Mary is in her sixties. She is still happily married to her second husband, but there is no one else. She was an only child, and her parents are both gone. It wasn't until recently that she started thinking about the prospect of being alone, the possibility of declining health or unforeseen expenses, and the desire for companionship, love, and grandchildren.

The choices she made in her twenties and thirties started to haunt her. Were those the right choices? Should she have taken a different path? Listening to the debates that take place today about pro-choice versus right to life, Mary began to wonder if she could do it over again, would she have done the same thing?

She reflected, "I certainly have had my share of guilt, a little regret from time to time, and a fair amount of second-guessing. From time to time, I even fantasize about what their lives would have become, but here's the truth. I always come back to the same conclusion. Knowing what I knew then, what options were available to me, and what was going on in my life at the times, I can say with certainty I would have made the same choices."

That was a stunning moment for Mary because it was the first time she had every really faced up to the question and definitively answered it with conviction—for herself.

One of the lessons from this interview is that we often put too much energy in looking back and second-guessing our choices. The harsh reality of life is that once you make a choice, you can't undo it. You can make a new choice, you can go a different direction in the future, but putting energy into regretting that original choice is of no value to you or anyone else. In fact, it can be quite harmful.

This was the epiphany Mary had as we were doing this interview. She said to me, "You know, I could spend the rest of my life playing the 'what if' game.

What if I had those children? What if I never married my first husband? What if I never met my second husband? What if those children grew up to be bright successful men or women? What if they had children of their own and I had grandchildren today? It doesn't matter, because that ship has sailed. It is never going to happen."

Mary cannot turn back the clock of time and change those choices. Based on her personal views, the circumstances of her life, her goals, and yes, her values *at the time*, she made choices that were right for her.

When I asked Mary what values she drew upon to make the choices she did, she became very introspective. Her values on the surface seemed to be guided by concern for others, reputation, and responsibility. But when she thought about it, she realized that she had been quite selfish in the choices she made. Her conclusion was that perhaps if she had dug deeper and approached her situations with core values like honesty, integrity, and love, she may have made different choices. And there would have been different consequences. When she looked back with objectivity, she admitted that her values of reputation, and responsibility as well as concern for others were used as shields to justify her actions.

But the bigger lesson in Mary's story is that choices made once cannot and should not haunt you for the rest of your life. We go through life trying to do the right thing and make the right choices. In the end Mary said, "Tell your readers to make the choice that is right for them—not for anyone else—and not because society imposed choice or a belief on you, but because it is the right choice for you at a moment in time based on the information you have at your disposal. Regardless of any choice you make, there will be consequences."

Mary went on to say, "I know people will judge me; heaven knows I have judged myself over the years. But that goes nowhere and serves no one, least of all me. I hope that by reading my story, others will take a bit more time to tap into their values when faced with a life-changing decision. When faced with a choice that has an irrevocable impact, pause to remind yourself that once you make it, it is a forever choice. If I had made different choices, my life would have been different but not necessarily better. I can't invest any more energy regretting those choices made years ago."

Mary is one of the loveliest, happiest, and most secure people I have ever met in my life. She has let go of second-guessing herself and realizes that the woman she has become, with the life she has today, is what she was destined to have and to live, and she wishes the same for you.

Mary's story is an awakening to explore the range of values we hold true and their weight on choices we make at any point in time. The attitudes about abortion are polarizing and subject to vigorous debate, especially today. When you are faced with a difficult decision, what values will you tap into to guide you to make the choice that is right for you? Only you can answer that question.

Sometimes choices are not as definitive as Mary's. They are not irrevocable, but rather they are part of a journey that begins at some point in our life and continues to weave through it, pulling us forward. For us to be open to our own self-discovery, we must clear our minds and hearts of the clutter and listen for the signs, watch for the signals, and tune in to the universe.

Catherine Carlisi's story began this way. "Many, many years ago, I led a pretty circumscribed life. The only career choices were nurse, secretary, or teacher. I wasn't used to looking at my life as having options. I got a typical job in a large, well-known corporation, but my life changed when I went to a conference and was introduced to the concept of *who we are and what we can be.*

"That one sentence changed my life. It was my introduction to the theory of NLP (Neuro-linguistic Programming.) I didn't know what to expect, but I started to do some research, and I got my company to sponsor me for their month-long training."

It was the beginning of a radically different trajectory of her life. "During that process, I also learned about Insight Seminars and their three-part program titled "The Awakening Heart, The Opening Heart, and Centering in the Heart." When I completed their training, everything fell into place. It brought heart-based thinking to NLP. It's thirty years later, and I still use those concepts every day in my practice."

As Catherine's life changed, her career needed to change too. She left her corporate job and took off around the country with the goal to learn everything she could from others in the NLP space. It fascinated her and there was a resonance that vibrated when she encountered someone who added to her growing knowledge of personal discovery and new ways to connect with people.

"I was on a plane reading a story about Bali in the airline magazine. As fate would have it, I was in Canada shortly after that and met a person putting a program together in Bali that touched on many of the principals I had been learning.

"I had no money and no job, but my choice was to go for it!" Catherine spent three months in Bali, and while the program was good, her personal transformation came from Bali itself. By living in a culture very different from the one she came from, she learned to see, listen, and adapt in new ways. "I learned to say *not yet* instead of no, and it opened me up to limitless possibilities. Just because you haven't done something or been somewhere, it doesn't mean you can't."

The Bali people live with openness and resourcefulness. Their joy in life comes from the sense of "who knows what tomorrow will bring?" For example, there is no word in the Bali language for art because they believe everyone is creative. Paintings are collaborative, with many different people contributing. When you hear hammering on a roof, it is in musical syncopation. Dance is an important part of life, but the Bali people are uncomfortable with applause. They believe you dance for God and yourself, not for the pleasure of someone else.

Embracing the element of playfulness also shaped Catherine's future. Bali people accept life as it is. They have a strong sense of community. It is not honorable to have more wealth than your neighbors. They help each other out.

The relationship between husband and wife is not the primary relationship in their society. Men have strong bonds with each other, and women are close with each other. Children are redirected, never reprimanded. They revere babies and old people, believing they either just came from God or are preparing to return.

Tattooed men do not believe they are tattooed forever, but only until they are cremated! And cremations are a celebration of food and music while the body is going up in flames.

"I share this with you because of the profound impact it had on me, and in turn, the impact I have had on others. It was through living in that culture and having the time to examine my beliefs that I really understood the magic of the human psyche."

When Catherine returned to Los Angeles, her sister picked her up at the airport, and she immediately saw the change. For the first time in Catherine's life, the attention was on her because of the light she was shining.

Catherine's story is in some ways a metaphor for the journey that each of us makes during our life on this planet. We may not have the opportunity to spend three months in Bali, but we all have the capacity to change.

"I tell people, when you have the opportunity to experience yourself in a different way, don't pass it up. Most people live too small; it's easy to get disappointed in life. You begin to expect that you need other people to make you happy. It's easy to become cynical and think that view of the world is reality."

In her coaching practice, Catherine tells clients that insight comes when you start discovering ways you undermine yourself. It is not until you come face-to-face with your saboteurs that you can move on to discover your true self. This starts by having non-traditional experiences. It may be as simple as trying the local cuisine in the town or country you are visiting rather than the chain restaurants. Take a vacation to a different place. Engage in conversation with people you don't know. Read a book or take a course on something completely out of your comfort zone.

Catherine admitted that for years she had lived a small, petty life. So when she said yes to the unknown, life became an adventure. And as her life blossomed and grew, her biggest revelation was that if she ever found herself unhappy again, she could do something about it. "Remedy is not in traditional places; you have to look someplace else."

As you are reading this story, think about the things you would like to change, experience, or examine. This could be the most important choice you make for yourself. Thinking it's too late for you is simply not true—regardless of your age.

"We give ourselves so many reasons not to celebrate ourselves. Maybe because it's uncomfortable or we feel others will judge us. But they are not you, and you shouldn't allow anyone to define your life."

Catherine's story about choices is a prescription for you. What are the critical elements you can draw upon to move you from where you are to where you want to be?

Let's get to some practical advice. Don't necessarily buy other people's definition of yourself. Give yourself the opportunity to be surprised and don't be afraid to redefine yourself. Once you do, you can no longer hold onto those limiting views anymore. By being the one to do things your friends would never consider doing, you break the shackles of traditional choices.

Trying new things helps free you from limiting beliefs and judgments you hold about others. If you were writing your life story, how would it read?

Catherine, like many of us, was painfully shy in high school. She said she only had five friends. When she went to college, she made a choice to be a different person and began acting like she had confidence. "I realize, looking back, that by assuming the role of the person I wanted to be (even though nothing had really changed; I was still shy), everything changed. People looked at me differently, spoke to me differently, and treated me with respect." That was long before she learned NLP or went to Bali.

Your challenge is to write the script for the person you want to become—and become that person by acting that part starting today. If you have ever been to a play, you know the experience of being captivated by a character on stage. You don't think about the actor playing a role because you are witnessing the truth of that performance. This is not to suggest that you go through life living a lie. Instead, change your mental programming to dispel those self-limiting beliefs: seeing yourself as a victim, mistaking wishful thinking for action, resisting change, or putting others first at the expense of yourself.

Another sage insight that Catherine shared is tuning in to the critical element of finding and being your true self. The first is authenticity—who you are when you are not trying to posture or pretend or defend yourself by masking who you are. The second is congruence—when who you are on the inside matches what you show to the world.

Catherine asks clients, "Are you a driver, a passenger, or cargo?" In other words, what role do you play every day in your life? And are you fully satisfied with that role?

She suggests some easy things you can start doing today to put yourself on a path to change your life. "You don't have to go to a foreign country. Instead, take a course; complete a personal assessment; go to meetup.com and seize the opportunity to connect with like-minded people. Get out of your routine by breaking the pattern of your everyday life. Join Toastmasters—it will boost your confidence in every area of your life. Take a day trip on a bus from your area to someplace new."

Catherine's personal story and advice would not be complete without looking at her values. She knows that what drove her was the belief that she is on this earth to be a helper, to do a service in the world. Early in life this didn't shine through in either her job or her relationships. It was only through her journey of self-discovery that she truly embraced her inner values and mission in life. Along with being a helper, Catherine is the epitome of compassion, curiosity, fun, kindness, self-respect, and unselfishness—values she lives every day. She believes that what we do every day has a ripple effect on others. Only by being intentional and thoughtful in her choices can she effect positive change.

"As we keep ourselves open to new possibilities and continue to redefine ourselves throughout our lives, we truly become 'timeless.' In my experience, much of aging has more to do with losing that 'spark of life' than it does with the number of years lived.

"For many, our comfort zones become more and more constricting and narrowly defined as we get older. If we counteract that tendency through new experiences and an effort to remain relevant, we can continue to find meaning and enjoy our lives until the very end. At least that's my plan!"

Self-discovery is not an event; it is a journey. It should not be painful; it should be joyous. By keeping an open mind and an open heart, we are ready for new discoveries. When we have the chance to make a choice to move in one direction or another, we never know exactly what the outcome will be. We make our decision based on what we think will happen or what we want to happen, but things rarely unfold like the pages of a well-worn script.

Whether you agree or disagree with Mary's decisions and whether you feel you would have the courage to fly off to Bali as Catherine did, it doesn't matter. For both of them, the choices they made were all part of their own self-discovery. They have no direct relevance to you other than as examples of how two lives unfolded based on important choices.

The first step in self-discovery is to get in touch with who you are now. Take time for yourself—away from the noise, the distractions, the responsibilities—and think about what matters to you. If you were to give your life a grade, would it be an A, a C+, or an F? And what do you base that on? As you review each element of your life—family, money, career, education, health, spirituality—what is working for you? What is in need of attention? Where would you like to start? Where would you like to end up? Start now to embrace your own path to self-discovery.

SPIRITUALITY

*I don't object to the concept of a deity,
but I'm baffled by the notion of one that
takes attendance.*
AMY FARRAH FOWLER, *BIG BANG THEORY*

WHEN YOU WERE growing up, did you spend any time in church? Did you go to Sunday school with your grandmother? Did your parents attend church, or did they have nothing to do with any religion at all?

Religion, at its core, is based simply on faith—the faith that there is more than mortal life, the belief in things unseen. Religion teaches you that there is a heaven or an eternal reward, the promise of what is to come after death. Many religions teach that there is some sort of hell or punishment if you don't follow certain beliefs. Religion also influences how we should act during our life on earth.

This chapter is not meant to be a discourse about Christianity or any other religion, but rather a dialogue on how spirituality affects people's choices and the values that guide their lives. In sharing our backgrounds and beliefs, our goals are to provide insights for how we deal with our own spirituality and offer an avenue for you to do the same.

Reflections by Alan:

I grew up in a small country church environment. My family attended a Baptist church, and for the most part I enjoyed it. It helped shape my values and the choices I have made in my life. As I have gotten older, much of my philosophy has shifted in this area, and I have seen this with many other folks as well, both younger and older. People have changed over the past few decades and have grown a little weary of church in some respects. They have grown callous or cynical toward organized religion. They wonder, "Is this really necessary? Is this really the way God and the Universe actually works? Is there proof? What should I believe?"

These are all individual choices. If you stop and think about it, most people follow the religion of their parents. Being born in the United States, Christianity has been the dominant religion along with Judaism, but there are many other religions as well—you just don't hear about them as much, depending on where you live. I have traveled to other countries where religion is essentially nonexistent. I have been to countries where Islam is a major religion and to other countries where voodoo is the religion of choice. When you were born as well as where you grew up are factors that influenced your religion and your faith and shaped the beliefs that were instilled in you.

There are changes going on in churches today. Many churches are slowly dying because they have fewer and fewer people attending their services and participating and contributing to the church. Depending on your attitude toward church—good, bad, or indifferent—whether you go to church or not, or whether you believe or not, one thing is true: Churches are businesses. Similar to any corporation, it requires money to keep the building running, pay the employed workers, and operate the various outreach programs.

Growth in many churches has slowed down. Why? Are they are diminishing because people are growing weary of constantly being asked to tithe? Is it because our busy lives do not allow time for worship? Or is it because the congregations no longer relate to the doctrinal dogma? In speaking with young adults in their twenties and thirties, it has become apparent that the "thou shalt nots" do not resonate with many of them. We have been told by some, "It seems that everything other than breathing is a sin! We just can't win!" A generation of freethinkers that want to challenge prevailing beliefs are not open to sermons or homilies that preach "don't do this and don't do that, or there will be consequences." (The consequences, of course, change depending on the religion.) The reality of life is that there are consequences, either good or bad, depending on the choices we make. (Stop paying the electric bill and see how long the lights stay on, for example.)

The concept of sin makes sense in principle, but when examples of immoral conduct occur in or around the church, the message is diminished. Stories about priests who abuse children, rabbis who commit massive welfare fraud, and ministers who swindle their congregations all contribute to the doubt and hypocrisy that drives congregations away. And then there are the headlines announcing parishioners involved in domestic abuse, opioid addiction, embezzlement, fraud, and drunk driving.

Reflections by Carol:

My birth mother was Catholic and my father was Methodist. The mother who brought me into this world died when I was six months old. When my father remarried, I was destined to be raised in the Methodist Church. My mother (the only one I ever knew) and I went to church every Sunday; I attended Sunday school, joined the Methodist Youth Fellowship, and sang in the church choir until I graduated from high school. All the rites were firmly engrained in me. The church was the center of my social life until I was old enough to have a social life of my own.

I believed in the Father, Son, and Holy Spirit, the Bible, sin, and salvation through Jesus Christ, as well as the teachings of sanctification, the sacraments of baptism, communion, confirmation, and holy matrimony. The church also taught belief in free will and social justice. I could recite the Apostles' Creed and the Doxology by heart. I sang the hymns and prayed with the congregation.

But I was also heavily influenced by other doctrines. My birth mother's family allowed me to understand and appreciate Catholicism. When we were together, I would go to Mass and witness the Eucharist, see the confessional, and watch while people lit candles in prayer for others. My two closest friends growing up were Jewish, one Reform and one Conservative. I was invited to seders to join in the celebration of freedom, watch the ritual of lighting candles each night of Hanukkah, and participate in each of their bat mitzvahs. Blending Protestant, Catholic, and Jewish influences, I became a bit of an ecumenical mutt.

It wasn't until I was finishing my freshman year in college that I began to question the church. And over the next couple of years, my faith was put to the test. Living in Washington, D.C., I witnessed political turmoil and triumph on Capitol Hill, protests against the Vietnam War, and the plight of frustrated demoralized returning veterans. I studied the awkward transition from Lyndon B. Johnson to Richard M. Nixon. Events that influenced me included Apollo 8, the first manned spacecraft to orbit the moon, and the Apollo 11 landing on the moon the following year. I watched the news as the assassinations of Robert F. Kennedy and Martin Luther King Jr. were reported and the loss of four college students at Kent State, gunned down by the Ohio National Guard. And, of course, anyone who lived during this time remembers Woodstock, the event that defined an era.

The dichotomy between my religious upbringing and the real-world events swirling around me contributed to my growing doubt about the role of religion and the goodness of people. During the summer between my sophomore and junior year, I was asked to deliver part of the sermon at my home church. I vividly recall the minister's and the congregation's reaction.

My message was that the church should not be a place where people go to hide out to declare or justify their faith. I challenged them to explore their own spirituality by how they conducted themselves in between the weekly sermons. I asserted that organized religion (of any faith) was merely a vehicle to defend and pardon those inexplicable phenomena in life that make us uncomfortable or unsettled. True faith and spirituality lay within each of us and should be expressed in our actions, not just our prayers and not just within the walls of the sanctuary.

I was not excommunicated from the church, but I wasn't invited to speak again from the pulpit. My revelation was that God was within me, and whether or not I went to church—any church—I was equipped to face the world with my brand of faith, spirituality, and values. Did those values come from the church? Of course they did, as well as from my parents, grandparents, and teachers.

As I have gotten older, I appreciate the influence that church had on me. It shaped my values, taught me right from wrong, and laid the foundation for the choices I make every day.

Those who try to be faithful are often faced with a moral dilemma: either "I can never measure up so why try?" or "If what they're preaching doesn't match their actions, why should I listen?"

Despite this grim picture, there is an important place in our society for church, synagogue, and temple. By bringing people together, a connection is welded in both faith and community. There is a platform to instill values and teach positive lessons when we stumble. Perhaps one of the benefits is social. Bringing individuals and families together for worship, kinship, and growth can and should strengthen our society.

Church can be a great resource for many people. It may be the social connection we all need. Beyond the ritual, churches are about helping people.

Sometimes just being with a group where you feel included, with people who share common beliefs, is enough to stem the doubt and loneliness we all feel from time to time. It reinforces the fact that you are not alone in the world and that each of us has a purpose.

Reflections by Alan:

There was a story about a man who had been going to church for a long time, but for one reason or another, he had not been to church in several months. He was well known at the church and had been very much involved for quite some time, so his absence was obvious to the congregation, and he was missed. The pastor stopped by one day to see him, and the man knew why he had come. It was wintertime, so they settled themselves in front of the fireplace where a pile of logs was burning. They sat there and watched the fire but didn't really say much of anything.

If you ever used a fireplace, you know you must stoke it and move the logs around to keep the fire going. After quietly sitting for a while, the pastor got up, and using the tongs, found a wood ember glowing bright red in the fire. He moved the ember away from the main part of the fire and set it down on the hearth. He then sat back down. Nothing was said. After a few minutes, the ember grew gray and cold as the heat diminished. It was slowly dying because it had been removed from the energy of the fire. When the ember appeared to be just about out, the pastor went back to the fireplace, picked up that ember with the tongs and put it back next to the fire. The ember began to glow again as it came back to life. It was gaining energy from the rest of the fire.

The pastor never said, "Hey, we miss you at church. Is everything OK? We'd really like you to come back." Moving the ember was all he did. The man understood the metaphor. When the pastor got up to leave, the man said, "Pastor, I'll see you next Sunday."

Sometimes I believe we put too much faith in the wrong things. And sometimes the church can seem to be merely a social gathering, especially to those who don't attend. However, I have found that church, in most cases, becomes an extended family that is there for you when you need it. I believe we all have a core need to belong, contribute, and be loved. Over the past twenty-plus years, I have spoken in over one hundred different churches. I have been in large churches with massive buildings, choirs, and congregations that have large initiatives for doing good things for the community. I have been in very small churches with only five to ten people who meet every Sunday, and they contribute more time and money to the necessary efforts than many of the larger churches. I even had one friend of mine say after a visit to a church, "I don't think the Lord has been in this church for a long time." Not all churches are the same. The people that make up the church are the difference. If you do believe, I urge you to find and attend a church, synagogue, or other spiritual center that feeds your soul.

Previously we mentioned Dan Miller of 48 Days. He tells a story using the phrase "praying with your legs." Essentially this phrase means that many people in the religious environment toss everything in God's lap. They say, "Well, it's up to God, and we'll see what happens." They pray over and over again for something thing to happen (or not happen), but with no results. After a time, they feel God is not hearing their prayer, and they assume God has forgotten them.

There is an old story about a man who prayed to God daily, asking to win the lottery. Every day this man prayed the same prayer. Whenever the lottery had a huge jackpot, the man prayed even harder. This went on for years. Finally, God had enough and said, "Look, I hear you. I have heard your prayer to win the lottery for the past ten years. But how about meeting me halfway? Go buy a ticket!"

If someone is sick, dying, or in trouble, I believe it is a good idea to pray for him or her. I think there is great benefit in the power of prayer. However, depending on the circumstances, praying without doing anything will not get you anywhere. I have seen many times on Facebook someone post about a death in the family or some other crisis. I then see multiple people respond by saying, "Praying." Do they actually stop and pray for that person, or do they just post to look good on Facebook?

That is the point of Dan's phrase "praying with your legs." My belief is that God is in everything, but God also expects us to be part of the program. It's one thing to get up every morning and say, "God, please help me through this. Please help me earn enough money this week to feed my family. Please help my car to start. Please let me get to work. Please give me a safe trip home." I do believe God looks after us and gives us the tools to cope with whatever conflicts may come our way. However, I still have to get up and do my part. God does the God part, but I am still part of the equation.

Sometime soon, go out, walk in the woods, and listen to all the birds singing. If you just take a moment to listen, they are all chirping and singing. There are birds everywhere. Have you ever wondered how they got there?

How do they eat? They all must feed on something. God provides all the animals with food. Berries, seeds, worms, and insects are all there for the taking. However, God does not deposit the food in the nests. The birds must get out of the nest and forage for food. They know instinctively that their very survival depends on it. In this particular case, the birds are praying with their wings.

My suggestion is to continue to pray for whatever circumstance you are dealing with. Pray what you need to pray. Show gratitude for what you already have. Ask God for what you need. Then shut up and be quiet. Calm you mind and listen. God rarely yells.

We have to get up, go out, and do our part. "Praying with your legs" is more powerful than just spending your time on your knees. Listen to yourself, and if you often hear yourself saying things like, "Well, if God allows . . . if God wills . . . if God tarries," you are shirking your responsibility and expecting God to make choices for you and do everything else too.

We believe that there is a higher power, an omniscient authority that exists beyond human life. No matter what your beliefs are, if you take a moment to be quiet and just listen, you may find that the universe, and perhaps God, is trying to tell you something. Our good friend Glenn Morshower calls it "listening to the whisper," paying attention to the message and trusting the message will guide you to do the right thing. Some people call it the voice in their head or the little man standing on their shoulder.

Learn to tune out the noise that assaults us every day. Turn off the radio and TV, put down the mobile phone and tablet, and find a place away from other people and distractions. Give yourself the time to get in touch with your own spirituality. It is in those quiet moments where inspiration, direction, and solutions make themselves known.

By tapping into your whisper, you will gain clarity around your true core values, and they will guide you to make sound choices.

SUICIDE

*Fall seven times
and stand up eight.*
Japanese Proverb

SUICIDE. THE WORD always conjures up the question, "Why?" Why would someone do this? Why would someone want to take his or her own life? Why would they leave their family behind this way?

Reflections by Alan:

I have been troubled by the idea of suicide for years. I had some friends several years back that have taken their own life for different reasons, and I've always struggled with that. I've always wondered what in their mind would cause them to pull the trigger or to put that rope around their neck or to take an overdose or stuff a rag into their tail pipe. Why? The answer is . . . I don't know.

I recently talked with Bob Donnell, a California suicide prevention counselor. For the past several years he has helped people decide against taking their own life. He told me that the idea of taking your own life comes from multiple different areas. In many cases, it has to do with drugs. It's far too common today for people to overdose. Drugs are readily available just about everywhere. In most cases, people overdose accidently. This is not really considered suicide, but the results are the same. They ended up killing themselves by taking too many drugs or ingesting a lethal combination of drugs and alcohol.

Many people in this country suffer from depression. Studies show there is no single answer for why people are depressed. Part of it is society. Part of it is their environment. It can be tied to mental illness or a painful upbringing.

For some, the time comes when they just feel that they can't go on. Many people are overwhelmed, and the tide of despair washes over them like a violent wave. They have too much work to do. They have too many responsibilities, too many people making demands on them. They may be struggling with the burden of providing for their families. Financial despair took on epic proportions during the stock market crash of 1929. People jumped from buildings and committed other acts of suicide because they had lost everything and were financially destitute.

But the real crisis in America is the rising level of teenage suicides among young people at the beginning of their lives who don't have the financial or work burdens that adults face. Besides drug abuse, what is causing this spike?

One of the major contributing factors is bullying. There are stories in the news every week about another teenager (or preteen) taking their life because they were bullied on Facebook or bullied at school. The cruelty that other kids exhibit because someone is too fat, too skinny, not pretty enough, or doesn't fit in with the crowd is a blatant example of poor choices and lack of values.

Our society is only now coming to terms with accepting homosexuality. Laws have been passed, churches are opening their arms, and businesses are no longer discriminating. But that is not universal. There are still many unresolved attitudes and biases that make it difficult for gay or lesbian or transgender men and women to cope. Adults have a fighting chance because they are better equipped to navigate the landscape. But think about teenage boy or girl who is just coming to terms with their sexuality. When there is even a hint that someone is gay, the bullying can be unmerciful and deadly. If parents don't know or are unsupportive, if the religious affiliation of their youth condemns homosexuality, or the teen has no one they can turn to for support, suicide can seem like the only option.

But there is a generation at the other end of the spectrum that may look to suicide as a way of ending their life. We are seeing more older adults commit suicide because they are facing terminal illness or a long and difficult journey with Alzheimer's disease. Doctors are divided on the issue, but our laws still make assisted suicide illegal in all but six states and Washington, D.C.

What can a patient and their family do? The patient wants to die with dignity; they don't want to be a financial burden; they don't want to be kept alive with drugs and machines, so they seek out ways to end their lives at a time and in a way that they choose.

Since this is the one choice in life that is completely irreversible, it is one that needs to be carefully weighed. I consider suicide as a permanent solution to a temporary problem. Obviously terminal illness is not temporary; Alzheimer's has no cure yet. But what if you went bankrupt? You lost the girl? You lost your job? Bad times for sure, but is it worth killing yourself? It is possible to learn from the experience and move on. Seek the help that is out there to get you through the crisis. And learn how not to get into those situations again.

Many people call suicide selfish. A person who commits suicide is just worried about their own problems and doesn't realize the pain they will cause for the people they leave behind. Bob Donnell told me that when someone has made up their mind to take their life, they will do it. He said usually there are signs in their mannerisms, in their talk, and in words that they use. If you are paying attention, you can see these signs. But if someone has truly made up their mind to end it all, there's almost nothing that you can do to talk them out of it.

I asked him about the religious aspects of suicide. Studies show that a religious person that attended religious services on a regular basis is less likely to commit suicide, even though they might be suffering from the same type of depression, drugs, or other issues. Religious services and being around others can help prevent suicide just by sharing and experiencing a more positive mind-set. Part of the reason may be the feeling of being part of a group where they feel valued. The most recent statistics find that suicide is the tenth leading cause of death in the US. Over 44,000 Americans die by suicide annually. And for every successful suicide, twenty-five other people have attempted it.

The risk factors that can lead to suicide are depression (and other mental disorders), substance abuse, prior suicide attempts, family history of suicide, family violence (including physical or sexual abuse), firearms in the home, incarceration, and bullying.

But thoughts of suicide aren't always induced by the more obvious things mentioned. Sometimes people are simply overwhelmed and don't know how to cope. In this busy world where we are slaves to the clock, pinged by our mobile devices, and woken up at midnight to check email, it's no surprise that the weight of it can become too much to bear. If you are one of those people or you know someone who is, then it's time to put up the stop sign. Take time out for yourself and help the other person do the same. And if you can't handle it on your own, do not be embarrassed about seeking help.

There are a variety of services, counselors, and resources available. Chances are there are family members you can reach out to for guidance or maybe simply for conversation. Find someone who will listen and guide you through whatever shark-infested waters you are treading. Do not make a permanent choice for what is most likely a temporary problem, or at least a treatable problem.

As mentioned earlier, many suicides are related to drugs. Recently I spoke with a law enforcement officer relatively new to the profession. He went to school with my youngest son. I asked if he would mind sharing what he has seen in the past year being on the force. He said it has opened his eyes to all the negative things going on that most people never see. One of the revealing parts of our conversation was about Narcan, an opiate antidote used to block the effects of opioids and reverse an overdose. Since police officers are often first on the scene in overdose situations, many law enforcement agencies are training officers to use Narcan to save lives.

He shared that as long as the person has not expired, Narcan works immediately to reverse the effects of the opioids. There is a catch, however. Narcan is very powerful, and the effect is so strong that often the victim revives in a state of rage and can become physically violent. They may think you are there to hurt them because you killed their buzz.

The opioid problem is so rampant now, though, that the directive from his superiors is shocking. In an overdose situation, if the person is a repeat offender, after the third time, the officers have been instructed to let them go—i.e., allow natural selection to take place. This is known as the Strike Three Rule: The first time someone overdoses, Narcan is free; the second requires the victim to fulfill some type of community service to help pay for the cost; and the third time, they may be left to die. And if the officer is by himself or herself, they are not to administer Narcan because the potential physical threat to the officer is too dangerous.

Another contributing factor to these new directives is that users are adopting the attitude, "I'll take this drug, and if I happen to OD, someone will find me, give me Narcan, and bring me back. I'm not going to worry about it if I happen to go a little too far." With drug users and law enforcement at odds over this issue, some jurisdictions are exploring other options.

Is the choice here suicide or assisted suicide? That's a debate that will probably go on for many years, but in either case, it is a choice. It should be obvious there is a battle of values underlying this issue. Personally, I find it very sad that drug use is so prevalent in our modern, sophisticated culture.

In speaking with a recruiter recently, she shared that at a job fair she attended, one company had thirty-five people lined up to apply for jobs. When the representative announced that there would be drug testing before anyone was hired, all but two got up and left. This is representative of how serious this crisis is and why preventing drug abuse needs to remain a top priority.

It is a slippery slope that can start with a few puffs on a joint, an experiment with cocaine or heroin, or even drinking alcohol. If someone is motivated to seek a better buzz, the outcome rarely ends up positive. Prescription drugs add a whole other layer of complexity to the subject.

What can you do? Pay attention to the people you hang out with, and when temptation is put in front of you, walk away. If the situation persists, find new friends. Have meaningful conversations with your doctor and your pharmacist about the possible effects of any drug being prescribed. Do your own research on prescription drugs and watch for side effects.

Remember, you are here for a reason. Do not mess that up! Have a good time, but don't have such a good time that it ends up being your last one.

Reflections by Carol:

Suicide and all it involves for the victim is a tragedy. But often for the family, it is even worse. When a person does commit suicide, their problems are over. But what and who have they left in their wake?

I remember my first experience with suicide. My real estate brokerage company shared office space with a law practice consisting of three lawyers. They were all highly successful and enjoyed fine reputations in the community. They were all married and had children they were proud of. The eldest attorney in the partnership was the first to send his only son off to college. I remember how proud he was when he brought the acceptance letter from Villanova to the office for us to see.

His son had always been a bright student but never the top of his class. He was an above average athlete but never the captain of the team. But in his father's eyes he was a superstar. Whenever the opportunity presented itself, he would bring his son to events just so he could brag on him. He would beam with pride whenever his son was around.

It was a Thursday morning when I got the call. The police had found his son's car in a parking lot behind the local supermarket. He had used rags to jam the tailpipe and a garden hose from the tail pipe through a slightly open rear window to fill the car with carbon monoxide. He was dead when they found him.

His father was never the same. Over the following weeks and months, I witnessed the collapse of a happy, vibrant, and successful man. He had lost his heart, his soul, and his very reason for living. His role in the practice evaporated overnight because he couldn't work. He started to drink, stopped shaving, and detached from all his friends and social activities. Ultimately his wife left him and went to live with her sister as the only way she knew to save herself.

The note left in the car said simply, "I'm sorry. I'll never be enough, and I don't have the strength to go on trying. I will only fail you, so I'm stopping it now."

There are no words of comfort, no easy solutions, no bounce back for the family of a suicide victim—only heartache, regret, guilt, and an extreme sense of loss.

Have you ever heard someone say, "I'm worth more dead than alive?" I did, and six months later that person took their life. They hung themselves in a closet and were found by their fourteen-year old daughter when she came home from school.

The wife never knew how much financial trouble they were in because her husband had always managed the money. They were deeply in debt, behind on their mortgage, and their family business attorney told her he had advised her husband to declare bankruptcy, but he was too proud.

The note he left behind said, "I cannot deal with it anymore, but my insurance will take care of you." The final blow came when the insurance company refused the life insurance claim because it didn't pay out in the event of suicide. For all the planning he did, he failed to read the fine print.

Their daughter went to therapy, but with limited results. She managed to graduate high school but didn't have the grades for college. She left home at eighteen to "find herself," and all she found was drugs and prostitution. No one knows where she ended up. She cut off all communication with her mother after she refused to post bail the third time her daughter was arrested.

These stories break your heart; they certainly broke mine, but they continue to happen every day. With every breath we take, we have another opportunity to make a new choice, a better choice. Once someone takes their life, all choices are snuffed out . . . for them and for those who love them.

The story we want to share in this chapter is from Paul. It involves a slower, agonizing, different type of suicide, but one with a tragic ending nonetheless. However, Paul's message is one of hope and reflection. By learning from his experience, maybe you will have the chance to help someone else who is in pain.

Relationships become complicated when two people love each other and want to be together, but life and careers get in the way. That is the foundation for Paul's story. The layers of complexity in this situation can only be described as daunting. While Paul was launching his career in marketing, he met Matthew, a college football player studying to be a guidance counselor.

The attraction between them was instant; however, both were coping with their own personal identity and finding their place in the world. Paul was outed in high school and had worked through the process of understanding and embracing his sexuality. Matthew was struggling with being true to himself while living up to the expectations of what his family, friends, and church believed about him.

Paul became the most important person in Matthew's life by supporting his journey, loving him unconditionally, and guiding him gently through the process of coming out. One of the key roadblocks for Matthew was the Catholic Church. He was raised to believe that homosexual acts are violations of divine and natural law. And his internal conflict was amplified by the fact that he had been sexually abused as a child.

After he graduated, he returned to his home state, over 1,500 miles from Paul. He was hired by a Catholic high school as their guidance counselor and football coach—not the place or roles that normally embrace a gay man. Paul was his rock; he was the only person in the world who Matthew could be honest with and who accepted him for who he was. Matthew was living two lives.

Over their eighteen-year relationship, they grew closer, but the miles between them made it difficult for them to fully commit to one another. They were in constant communication by phone and would visit each other as often as they could. Both men were balancing their careers, their families, their identities, and their love for each other.

Paul was in a near-fatal car accident in 2010, and Matthew flew immediately to be by his side. After his long recovery and months in rehab, Paul proposed to Matthew in 2011. They agreed that a long engagement was what they wanted. It allowed Matthew to remain closeted and retain his career as a Catholic school teacher and worship coordinator.

As Paul's health improved, he returned to his work as a Protestant minister and moderator of the Affirming Church, Welcoming Congregations, and Reconciling Ministries Coalition. "Most of the time I remained silent with Matthew on anything related to Catholic LGBTQ matters in the Roman Catholic Church. I educated myself on all sides of the issues, but I found myself walking on eggshells with my fiancé."

While this may seem like a complicated story already, there are other layers that both men were dealing with. Paul is white, and Matthew is black. Paul is bipolar and disabled but openly seeks support and therapy. He encourages others to be open about the challenges they face and is very proactive in deepening his own understanding and skills on issues such as suicide prevention, first aid, and awareness. He works tirelessly with the LGBT community doing advocacy work with affirming churches, as well as with Ugandan refugees seeking asylum.

Matthew's public persona was that of a proficient counselor and skilled athletic coach with a happy and fulfilled life. The other Matthew was a troubled man who blamed the Church for introducing him to "the life" and struggled to keep his family, friends, and colleagues from knowing the truth. "His ambiguity caused me concern, especially as it was accompanied by an increase in drinking while he was using the antianxiety medication Klonopin. On top of this, he had gastric sleeve surgery to reduce his weight and help ease the burden on his heart."

"I pleaded with him to stop drinking and to discuss his medications with his doctors, but I doubt I had much influence on his behavior. Due to my accident, I could no longer travel, so I was unable to be there for him. I threatened to discuss it with his family but never carried through. His family was still in the dark about his sexuality."

Everything up to this point represents a litany of choices made by both Paul and Matthew. But the choice that Paul made that brought everything to a crescendo was the choice of intervention.

The men talked frequently but only by phone now. It was apparent to Paul that Matthew was in crisis. He had already had multiple health scares. Everything he drank or swallowed compromised his heart problems and the benefits of the gastric sleeve. He was not supposed to drink or binge eat. For a self-proclaimed foodie, the mere idea of cutting back on food was the ultimate sacrifice. The surgery worked for a while, but ultimately Matthew turned to drinking to get his calories while he was taking the antianxiety drugs for his depression. Paul knew he was in complete denial of the seriousness of his actions, but he felt powerless to help.

One night Paul called Matthew and found him incoherent and disoriented. Paul decided to call the police in Matthew's town because he felt he couldn't call his family. They knew of Paul but still had no idea of the real relationship. "The police told me that reporting a false claim was a felony and questioned how I knew he was in distress. I was shocked, but I stayed firm until he got the help he needed that night. The police found him, took him to the hospital, and had his stomach pumped."

Sadly, it only had a short-term effect. Matthew died from another overdose a few months later. Looking back, Paul wishes he had persevered in getting him help. "I should have reached out to his family regardless of the consequences. I should have found a way to get him counseling. I should have been there."

Sometimes we make choices that are incomplete; they don't go far enough. We try with all our hearts to do the right thing, but something stops us from going that extra step. The ache Paul feels in his heart and the loss that still haunts him stems from that incomplete choice. His message is for anyone who knows a person in serious distress. "If I could replay those agonizing months leading up to his death, I would have done so much more. I would have found a way to intervene without ever disclosing the facts of our relationship; without jeopardizing his career or his relationship with his family."

With all that has happened, Paul realizes that the underlying value that drove him was compassion. "I really cared for Matthew and wanted the best for him. I was trying to be respectful of his family. But in doing so, I failed him by not going the extra mile when he couldn't do it for himself."

Perhaps Paul's compassion, as well as his own self-determination to combat the demons of being bipolar and learning to live with a new physical disability, masked his ability to see that Matthew could not cope by himself until it was too late. When we possess certain values that are crystal clear to us, we often miss the signals that others don't have the same commitment or internal belief systems and therefore won't respond in the way we expect.

Paul is a gentle giant; a shining example to anyone of how to cope with adversity with dignity and an unflinching spirit. There are no words to express our deep gratitude to him for sharing this raw and painful story. It has made him even stronger and more determined to help others while he continues to help himself.

WHEN DISASTER STRIKES

Courage is not having the strength to go on;
it is going on when you don't have the strength.
THEODORE ROOSEVELT

WHAT DISASTER HAVE you faced in your life? Not to be pessimistic, but if you haven't faced a crisis, it's only a matter of time. That's part of life. And the interesting thing is that, no matter how diligent you are about keeping your life in order, you are never fully prepared when disaster strikes.

Disaster can come in many forms. You can lose your house in a flood, a hurricane, a tornado, or an earthquake. Your business can be destroyed by fire or theft or an unexpected seismic shift in the market. Your personal life can be turned upside down in an instant when someone is in an accident or diagnosed with a terminal illness, you lose your job, or your spouse announces they are leaving you.

You seldom see it coming, and it will knock you off your feet . . . as least for a while.

We often ask our audiences, "Is there anything you just couldn't get through?" Invariably, they look at us inquisitively, not quite sure what to say. The truth is, if you are alive today, right here, right now, you have made it through all the toughest times you have ever faced so far. Those times may have been soul crushing, but yet you are still here. You are stronger than you think.

Listening to a recent promo with Lester Holt, news anchor for NBC *Nightly News*, reminded us how resilient we are as human beings. Here's what he says: "This job allows me to see people sometimes at their most vulnerable. They've been through calamity, something horrible, but time and time again you see them move forward. And that, to me, is remarkable. If there's nothing else I've learned from this business, it's the ability of people to bounce back. To be at their lowest, their most vulnerable, and somehow put one foot in front of the other and move on. It is something remarkable to behold."

Those inspiring words make sense when you are talking about someone else. But when it's happening to you, what strength do you draw on and what choices will you make? Do you have uncompromising values that will guide you back to center? And what if the direction you choose to go conflicts with someone else?

If you were born before 1990, chances are you remember where you were when you heard the news on September 11, 2001. The morning anchors on the East Coast needed only seconds after the plane hit the second tower to announce that we were under attack. And the additional news from the Pentagon and central Pennsylvania sent the entire country into a state of panic and despair. It was surreal and, to some, felt like Armageddon. As a country, we were shaken to our core.

One of the stories that came out in the years following 9/11 was about a man on one of the upper floors of the North Tower. The building had been struck, and no one knew what was happening or what to do. The safety people from that floor instructed, "Stay here. Help is on the way. Stay calm. Stay on this floor."

The voice inside that man was screaming, "Get out!" Everything in him told him to leave. He asked others if they wanted to go with him. He told them, "I'm getting out of here. I'm not staying." They all decided to stay.

He descended from over fifty floors up, fighting smoke and debris on his way down. The lower he went, the more crowded the stairwell became. People were scrambling down while firefighters were ascending. It was total chaos.

He was more than halfway down when he saw a woman just sitting huddled on the stairs. She was a large woman gasping for breath and curled up in fear. He stopped, "Come with me. I'll help you. Let's get outside."

Her response was, "No. Go ahead without me. I just can't make it."

He answered, "Yes you can. It will be fine. I will help you, but you have to work with me."

She finally agreed, and they continued down together. She had trouble navigating the stairs, and it slowed him down, but they kept going and made it to the lobby.

When they came out of the stairwell, the entire lobby was filled with people—some tenants of the building, more safety people, firefighters, and policemen. The noises coming from above were deafening. Through the windows, they could see debris and bodies hitting the pavement. The scene and the sounds were truly horrific.

The authorities were trying to maintain order and instructing people to stay in the lobby where it was safe so they wouldn't be hit with flying debris. The voice inside the man said, "No, you've got to get out."

He grabbed the woman by the arm and pulled. "Come with me. We must keep going."

She pulled back. "No. The security people say it's best to stay here. I can't go any farther."

He dropped her hand but said urgently, "Please come with me. I want to leave. I'm not staying here."

She stood firm. He said, "I have to go," turned, and walked out of the lobby. He was barely two blocks away when the tower collapsed. He ran for his life from the dust, debris, and ash that swept over the streets.

He survived. The woman he assisted down all those flights of stairs did not. She died in the lobby of the North Tower. The question is, did he make the right choice? Did she make the right choice? Did she decide to die that day, or did he decide to live?

The power of this 9/11 story is in the man's inner voice. We all have one. But do you listen to yours? Your inner voice is your most powerful guide. Remember, our friend Glenn Morshower calls the voice your "whisper." He believes that tuning in, paying attention, and heeding the direction of your own inner voice will never lead you the wrong way. It may not always make sense at the time, but it is never wrong. Our inner voice is our strongest advocate for survival, for success, for doing what's right.

But doing what's right and knowing how to deal with disaster isn't easy. No disaster when it befalls us comes with a handbook of "How to Get Out of This Mess." We have to do it on our own. We decided to take a different turn in this chapter after our 9/11 story. Sometimes lessons about how to cope can best be learned from absurdity. We have a good example of that.

Maybe you remember the 2003 movie with Jim Carrey called *Bruce Almighty*. It was a story about a news reporter in Buffalo, New York, with a stalled career and generally discontented with almost everything in his life, despite his popularity and the love of his girlfriend Grace. After a particularly bad day, he rages against God, accusing him of not doing his job. God, played by Morgan Freeman, responds by appearing in human form and endowing

Bruce with all his divine powers. He challenges him to take on the big job to see if he can do it any better.

The two rules Bruce must follow are 1) he cannot tell anyone that he has God's powers, and 2) he cannot use the powers to interfere with free will. As you might expect, Bruce ignores God and sets out to use his newly found powers for personal gain. Suffice it to say, things do not go smoothly for Bruce.

He manages to get the job as news anchor but loses his girlfriend in the process. In the meantime, he begins to hear voices in his head. God appears again and explains what he is hearing are people's prayers and he must deal with them. Bruce creates a system to receive and respond, but the influx is so great that he sets the program to automatically answer yes to every prayer.

He continues to focus on his own selfish needs, but he can't get his girlfriend back because he cannot interfere with her free will. He realizes that automatically granting everyone's prayers has created chaos in Buffalo, so he reaches out again to God, who tells him he must figure out a way to solve this himself.

We'll let you watch the movie to fill in the details, but we would like to share a deleted scene from the DVD that was not in the movie.

The deleted scene goes something like this: God takes Bruce to a place where he projects a video on a large wall to show Bruce why he doesn't answer yes to everyone's prayers. One example was a young boy who was asking not to be bullied or beaten up anymore. Bruce, being God at the time, said yes, so the other kids stopped bullying him.

God explained that he was not trying to punish the boy, but when Bruce said yes and stopped the bullying, he took away some of the pain and suffering that the boy needed to go through to become the great poet he was destined to be. The soul of his work would have been built around all that childhood pain. Instead, Bruce changed the course of the boy's life, and he was now headed for a career as a professional wrestler. God told Bruce he would eventually test positive for steroids and end up managing a muffin shop.

This brings up the question about how we react and what we wish for when bad things happen in our life. Do you wish for things to change, to get better, or do you stand up and face adversity, making difficult choices when things are at their worst? Is it even possible to be able to accept that there may be a higher power or a greater purpose behind what's happening?

We have all gone through tough times in our lives. Alan was laid off from three different jobs during his career at a time when he had a young family to support. Was it scary? Yes. Carol has been through a divorce, been fired from a job, and lost a home to fire. Was it difficult? Yes. But we are both still standing today, here to tell our story and hopefully inspire others.

At the time and in the moment when bad or even tragic things happen to us, it's easy to see nothing but the bottom of the pit. There seems no easy way out. But when your only choice is to power through, putting one foot in front of the other, amazing things happen. New doors open, and opportunities present themselves. The trick is to make the choice to take that first step. Do not waste time wallowing in self-pity or regret.

There is truth in the wisdom that hindsight is 20/20. It may be months or even years later before you see the value or the lesson of the experience. This is what makes us stronger; it makes us better people and provides us with the wisdom to make the right choices in the future.

PART TWO

FIRST MAJOR CHOICES

*Good habits formed at youth
make all the difference.*
ARISTOTLE

IT SHOULD BE obvious by now that making choices, especially ones that are going to move us in a positive direction, is no easy task. As adults, we have the benefit of time, knowledge, and experience to help us make wiser choices. But what about our young adults? We still have authority over our children until they reach the age of maturity, but once they turn eighteen, the law sees them differently, and they see themselves differently (even if their parents don't).

There is an imaginary line that gets drawn in the sand which demarcates where parental choices end and the choices of our sons and daughters take over. We don't want them to make mistakes, but how will they learn if they don't? We have to trust that everything we have done up to that point has prepared them to take over the reins of their lives. The safety net is removed, the harnesses are untethered, and it's time for them to fly on their own.

Now, before you go into cardiac arrest, we are not suggesting that you abandon your children. You should always be there to support them in a time of need, and you should always be available to lend an ear when they come to you for advice. We are simply saying that you have to allow them to make their own choices.

Let's take a step back and look at a few situations that lend insight into the types of things that influence the capacity of young minds to make choices for themselves.

- When you see, hear, or know of something that is going wrong—maybe someone is running a meth lab in the basement next door. You know it, but you turn a blind eye.

- You know through a confidential conversation that someone is being abused, but you don't do anything about it to help them get out of that situation. You just listen.
- When you know a teen was in a hit-and-run accident, you recognize the description of the car, you see the damage to the car, but you don't call the police because your relationship with the teen's parents is too important to you—they are your business clients.

Whenever you adopt the attitude that it's not your business to interfere or get involved, it's an example of the elasticity of your values and demonstrates how firmly your belief system is rooted to always do the right thing. Your children are watching and learning.

When a mother has a drink or two and then puts her children in the car, straps them in, and drives down the highway, for whatever reason (it doesn't matter), she's making a choice. The question becomes whether it is merely a lapse in judgment or a poor choice that made her think that having a couple of drinks was no big deal. Or is the problem deeper than that? If she *truly* loved her children and knew that, no matter what, she would make the right choice for their well-being, would she have made a different choice? Of course she would have. It's obvious. So, what happened?

And where did she go wrong? Was it her commitment? Was it the drink? Was it feeling that she was OK to drive and didn't have to arrange other transportation? Or was it a rationalization that she wasn't drunk and she was only going a short distance?

Unfortunately, in situations like this people tend to repeat the same behaviors over and over again, each time pushing the envelope a little further. Two drinks become three; the short distance becomes a longer distance . . . until finally something tragic happens.

When teens make a choice to text while they drive, or they drive drunk, or they leave the scene of an accident, how are they held accountable? What lessons do they learn? What values were instilled in them at a very young age for them to make such poor decisions? We all know that teenagers push the envelope of what their parents tell them. Peer pressure kicks in, along with the thrill of independence and that youthful attitude that it might happen to somebody else but it will never happen to them. Could values have made a difference? Maybe.

When you think about it, not every single teenager drinks and gets behind the wheel. Not every single teenager insists on texting while driving. Not every single teenager makes poor decisions. What is the fundamental difference? Is it the foundation of their values? Is it their fear of the consequences? Maybe it was a life-changing experience when one of their friends had a fatal accident, and they now have a different perspective. Or maybe it's as simple as that what they saw and heard as a child from the backseat translates to repeated behavior when they take over the wheel.

There's a simple answer to all of this. But we know that the answer does not apply to everyone in all situations. People think differently. People respond differently. People react differently. Consider this:

Have a dialogue with your children about values and what really matters—as individuals, with family, with friends, in the workplace, in the community, in the church, in the state, in the country, and in the world. Values apply at every level of human interaction. And by the way, they also apply in non-human interaction. Some people's values guide them to a belief system that a dog's life or a cat's life or a squirrel's life is as valuable and important to the universe as a human life. Others have no regard for animals. They abuse them, they train them to fight, they neglect them, they kill or torture them, and then they laugh. When you hear it on the evening news, you wonder what is wrong with people like this. They don't care–but why?

Where was that left out of the lesson plan? When fathers, uncles, or brothers abuse a child in their family, where were they when that was being discussed at the dinner table? In Sunday School? Or on the playground? And the real tragedy here is that because of some people's lack of or very distorted views of values, this gets passed on to future generations. The abused child grows up seeing the world differently through no fault of their own, but through a fearful, defensive, cynical, and sometimes hostile viewpoint. Because they've seen the evil side of life, they lose faith in whatever values they might have had. They don't think they mean anything, and without a strong belief in values, poor choices are bound to occur.

The examples we set as adults, the open dialogue we allow to discuss issues in the news or family concerns, and the deeper discussion about how and why choices were made and what values stood behind those choices will empower your children in unimaginable ways as they venture out in life.

Reflections by Alan:

When you are young, you want everything fast. You want it now, now, now. Even grown adults want everything immediately in this microwave society we live in today.

What happens when you marry your high school sweetheart? It's not unusual for young people who grew up together and have shared the same background to gravitate to each other when the hormones start raging. This new view of each other is often tied to physical attributes that weren't there before. The desire for sex is often confused with love and can open the door to some really bad choices.

Some will end up pregnant first and then head straight to the altar. Others, because of religious influence, may defer sex but still rush to get married to remove that barrier. Either way, choices are being made without much experience and for the wrong reasons. Statistics are grim for teenage marriages.

- Only 54 percent have a chance of their marriage lasting ten years.
- Waiting until age twenty-five increases the ten-year success rate to 78 percent.
- Only 19 percent of people who marry their high school sweethearts attend college.
- Less than 2 percent will earn a college degree.

We live in promiscuous times. The clothes teenagers wear, the music they listen to, the movies they watch, and the role models they admire all contribute to conflicting views of love, marriage, sex, and self-worth.

We sometimes see people getting married too young because they feel the only way they can have sex is to get married. Because they are young and they don't have much life experience yet, that's the choice they make. It's based on the values that were instilled in them by their parents and other adults in their world.

What happens in many cases, when these young people get married, everybody is happy. The church is happy. Their friends are happy. The families are happy... well, usually. So now they are married. They go on their honeymoon, if they can afford one, and they start living together. They set up house and everything is wonderful. What could possibly go wrong? Over the first year or two, though, the honeymoon phase fades. The mystique disappears in the relationship because they now see each other every day and deal with each other in much different ways than when they were only dating. They have chased each other around the house naked. They have had sex in every room of the house, scaring the cat and dog. They have seen each other naked a thousand times. They have burped and farted in front of each other. They have been sick in front of each other. They have woken up with no makeup on and morning breath. They don't wear their best outfit for a date anymore, and more often than not, they live in their sweatpants and ratty T-shirt. So many of the things that attracted them to each other have faded just a bit.

This young person wakes up, and now they are twenty-three years old. They realize that, according to their religious beliefs, they are going to be married to this one person for the rest of their lives. In reality, they just wanted to have sex. Now they wonder, "Is this really what I wanted? Is this really the person I want to spend the rest of my life with?" And in far too many cases, they discover too late that they married too soon.

This raises many questions, especially if you come from a conservative religious environment. I'm not encouraging young people to jump into bed with anybody and everybody before they get married, but once a person makes the choice to marry young, they can't turn back time. My advice to young people is to be very cautious about who they get involved with and don't jump into marriage quickly, because marriage is meant to be for a lifetime. It's one of the biggest life decisions we will ever make because most people anticipate only getting married once. So we need to think long and hard before tying the knot.

If you know anything about the Amish, their way of life seems very foreign to us and rather backward. Perhaps it is. On the other hand, everyone seems to know his or her place. There are questions about whether that's good or bad, and I'm not here to argue that. The boys and girls grow up together; they all go to school until what would be considered the eighth grade. At that point, the boys go off and begin learning a trade. It may be furniture making or farming. Obviously, it is some sort of rural trade. For the girls, their course of action is always, 100 percent of the time, to become homemakers.

Amish young people don't begin dating until they are in their late teens to early twenties. Most of them get married relatively young. They usually stick together for the rest of their lives and have large families because that's the way they were raised; these are their values. Some people see all this as very backwards, while others see it as secure and calming; they feel there is an order to their lives.

Young people are a lot smarter today than when I was growing up, at least from a technology and informational standpoint. We can Google just about any question we want and find an answer. This doesn't necessarily make young people wiser, however. That's where life experience comes in. And believe me, life can be messy. We hope young people reading this book will use this information we've presented to make better choices for their relationships.

Yes, it's possible to fall madly in love at first sight. I've known people who have met, dated for three weeks, got married, and are still married twenty years later. I've heard stories of people who knew each other growing up. They dated for ten years, got married, and the marriage didn't last six months. You never know! It's important pay attention and think through all this. My advice is to follow your heart, but use your head.

It is so easy to underestimate or ignore the wisdom of our children. In our efforts to root out what they are thinking about and what questions they have as life unfolds before them, we decided to go right to the source. We posed four questions to a variety of young people ranging in age from eighteen to twenty. This audience is on the cusp of independent adulthood and preparing to face their own choices. The trends are undeniable, and their responses may surprise you. Each one responded on paper with no request for identity other than age. Each bullet point represents a response from a different person.

What do you wish you knew one to five years ago that might have made your life better?

- I wish I would've known that everyone's heart isn't pure.
- I wish I knew that everything is not set in stone and things change. Also, that you can't change everything because some things are not how they will be.
- Don't stress yourself out trying to succeed. You will be successful if you enjoy life.
- That happiness can't be found from an outside source if you can't find happiness in yourself.
- I wish I spoke at least two other languages, could play an instrument like a violin, harp, or piano, and knew how to study better. I wish I knew how to deal with my health better. And I wish I had an emotional support pet and could go to a school that supports them.
- I wish I knew that every single choice I make today will eventually affect tomorrow.
- I wish I had known that connecting with friends is a better solution for dealing with stress than smoking weed.

- I would like to have known myself more, and I would still like to keep discovering myself.
- I wish I could have understood the big picture—that not everything lasts forever.
- I wish I knew the importance of being more responsible in my choices.
- I wish I had known that your past does not define you.
- I wish I knew how to deal with and cooperate with people more properly.
- I wish I knew that you cannot get everything you wish for every time. At some point, you have to realize that, no matter how good you are, you cannot succeed.
- I wish I knew that having a job in high school can really help you.
- I wish I knew that other people's opinions do not matter.
- I wish I knew how important education is to leading a successful life.
- I wish I knew that working hard pays off and laziness doesn't accomplish anything.
- I wish I knew the importance of good study habits and I wish I had been more motivated.
- I wish I would have known the impact drugs would have on my life.
- I wish I'd known that I wasn't as grown up as I thought I was.
- I wish I wouldn't have been so mean to my parents.
- I wish I could have spent more time with my parents and less with my so-called friends.
- I wish I would have chosen better friends.

What do you wish you knew more about? (money, relationships, travel, work, life)

- I wish I knew more about what I needed to do to get where I want to be.
- I wish I knew more about life. For example, what will happen later in my life?
- I wish I knew where God plans for me to be.
- I wish I knew more about how people live in other countries. It would help me appreciate what we have here.

- I wish I could travel. I want to know more about how people work—relationship-wise.
- I wish I knew more about jobs and what my best options are for my future.
- I wish I knew more about self-value and my relationship with me—loving being me.
- Money, relationships, travel, work, and life. I wish I knew more about all of those things.
- I wish I knew more about myself, life, and psychology.
- I'm undecided—I think that everything happens for a reason and I wish I knew what I needed to know about at the time.
- I wish I knew more about relationships and life in general.
- I wish I knew more about work and different aspects of careers.
- I wish I knew more about all the things listed.
- I wish I knew more about friendship, and good ways to save money.
- I wish I knew more about life and saving money.
- I wish I knew more about relationships because it builds when we grow from a small child to the big age person (above sixty-five to seventy) and all those years ahead as a father, mother, grandparent, husband, and wife.
- I wish I knew more about choosing the right friends and romantic relationships.
- I wish I knew how to build and maintain relationships, stocks and investments, and saving money.
- I wish I knew more about money. I continue to discover how truly ignorant I am when it comes to fiscal issues. I recently took out a loan at my bank, and it was quite the learning experience.
- I wish I knew more about life, money, and relationships.
- I wish I knew why these things are important.

What do you wish your parents had explained to you?

- I wish my parents would've explained how I could get to where I want to go with my life.

- People. I learn about people through observation. I would have loved to learn or get insight on people at a younger age because I feel I would know more now.
- I wish my parents had told me that not everyone will like you, but just enjoy yourself and be yourself. I wish I had been told I don't need negative people in my life.
- I wish my parents had told me about tax and money allocation at a young age. I wish they had explained the difference between Republicans and Democrats. I feel that people don't really know what they are; they just hear the names and choose what their parents choose.
- I wish my parents had taught me to manage my health better.
- I wish they had taught me how to be organized, and I wish they had made me work.
- I wish they had explained the importance of finding yourself, rather than just finding a way to make a living.
- I wish they had shared the importance of being yourself and how important you are to yourself. That no matter what happens, you are more important than anyone else. The big picture.
- Nothing. They explained everything . . . I just didn't listen.
- That it's OK to take advice. You don't have to experience everything for yourself. And that there are always positive or negative consequences that will or could follow you for life.
- I wish my parents would have explained what life would be like ahead.
- My parents explained about the good and bad around us. I wish they would have explained their own interests and what happiness means to them.
- I wish my parents had explained more about the real world and the fact that there are problems in every step we take.
- I wish my parents told me more about conducting myself in job interviews.
- I wish my parents had explained how to manage my money in college.
- I wish my parents had explained about their struggle in life at an early age.

- I wish they had told me how important it is to save your money.
- My parents pretty much explained the importance of education. I wish they stressed more about how to be a good friend and keep friends.
- I wish my parents had been more involved in teaching me about financial responsibility.
- I wish they had explained how to balance work, leisure, and studies all at once while in college.
- I wish they told me just how to stay above water.
- I wish my parents had explained that people aren't always what they say they are. Also, that not all people have good intentions.

What would do if you knew you could not fail?

- I would teach lessons to everyone in the world through music that they would carry with them throughout their lives.
- I might take more risks, but thinking about failing brings about failure.
- I would start my dream business designing signs.
- I would teach abroad and live happily in another country.
- I would own a sports team.
- I would sing and make my own music or become a motivational speaker.
- I would fly.
- I would push myself harder.
- Undecided.
- I would be a better person toward others.
- I would get my record expunged.
- I would be a surgeon and make large amounts of Benjamins.
- Maybe I would try to make things; work a little harder.
- I don't know.
- I would not try or work hard if I knew that could not fail.
- I would finish school and go to graduate school.

- I would play football forever.
- I would apply for scholarships and internships.
- I would follow my dreams; become a pastry chef or a YouTube sensation.
- I would be an author.
- If I knew I couldn't fail, I would become a PR specialist for a Fortune 500 company.
- I would finish school and go to law school.
- I would get my PhD. I would travel the world and just get life experience and help everyone I could.
- I would spread the gospel of Jesus Christ to the untouched parts of the world.
- I would be the owner of a Fortune 500 company.
- I would create the social network to replace Facebook.

What do all these answers show us? That our young adults have very mature insights into life, but they also recognize that their knowledge and experience is incomplete. They are not fully prepared for the future, and if they could turn the clocks back and fill in some of those gaps, they would feel more prepared.

As adults, we all share a responsibility to educate, inspire, encourage, and support our youth. They want honesty, and they seek the tools to make them strong. While they may not always listen, and they may even rebel, that does not give us an excuse to stop trying. The words of wisdom, caution, and truth will bury themselves deep in their hearts and souls, and those tapes will run automatically in their heads when they need them most.

REGIONAL INFLUENCES

What you think, you become.
What you feel, you attract.
What you imagine, you create.
        BUDDHA

DO PEOPLE MAKE choices based on where they grew up or where they spend most of their adult life? We would argue that yes, there are generalities that seem to exist even in our melting-pot country where people move more frequently and often experience different regions. Whether you are from the Southeast, the Northeast, the Midwest, or the West, it is fair to assume you have within you at least some of the admittedly stereotypical traits associated with that region. Regional differences tend to be reflected through in attitudes (and actions) associated with politics, religion, work ethic, family, and religion.

Please do not be offended by our descriptions for each region of the country. These are admittedly broad generalizations; there are always exceptions, but it is interesting to look at the well-established patterns to see how they influence choices and highlight values.

There is a term called "southern hospitality." Some see that definition as flattering, and others feel it is degrading. People who grew up and live in the southeastern part of the United States usually come across as friendlier, more open, and more willing to help than those in other parts of the country. They are known for having a kinder, friendlier, more laid-back attitude. At the same time, some people look at the folks from the Southeast as unsophisticated and naïve. For some the divide between conservative values and commitment to God and country are at odds with pockets of the South that still adhere to rigid views about racial relations. There is a tendency to hold on to the status quo and resist change or growth. Southerners tend to make choices with slow deliberation based on conservative Christian values.

The Northeast is by far the most congested area of the country, and when populations cluster together, everything moves at a faster pace, including choices. If you have ever been to Boston, New York, Philadelphia, Baltimore, or Washington, D.C., you get the picture. Even beyond the city limits, the surrounding suburban areas take on the frenzied characteristics. The farther north you go into New England or west away from the coast, the more you experience a calmer atmosphere. In the more congested areas in or close to the cities, life is usually centered around careers, making a living to support a higher cost of living, as well as cultural activities, sports, and education. People are driven and highly competitive. Choices are often made quickly, and the underlying values vary greatly.

In the Midwest, even in the larger cities like Chicago, Minneapolis, or Detroit, family and community are high priorities. There is a slower pace of life than you find on the coasts; people are genuinely friendly, and they look out for each other. Good manners and polite conversation are the norm, and there is an unspoken code of honor among Midwesterners to "do what's right." Choices are approached with serious consideration, a desire for adequate information, and the trust that the outcome will lead to positive things. Midwestern values such as fairness, friendship, community, kindness, respect, and citizenship are often expressed openly and reinforced through action.

The West represents a wide variety of cultures, backgrounds, geography, and opportunity. Because of that, defining the Western part of the U.S. is more challenging. Away from the coast, the pace of life is dictated by the geography around you. In a day's drive, you can go from mountains to plains and deserts, or to lively cities like Las Vegas. Outdoor activities and making a living off the land is the norm in vast areas of the West, so choices there are often influenced first by survival. Hard work and stability along with appreciation for adventure and nature's beauty are foundational blocks for western values. When you reach the West Coast and denser populations, there is an intensity, but it's very different than the East Coast. No matter where you go along the Pacific coastline, you find a heightened sense of concern for the environment and an easier-going attitude about life in general. That is not to say that people are not competitive. Just go to an open-call audition at any studio in Hollywood, and you'll witness competition that rivals the Olympics. There is a perception that people from the West (specifically California) are not authentic, do not play fair, and have their own moral code. Perhaps in some cases that's true, but you will also see plenty of evidence of courage, self-discipline, commitment, self-improvement, and determination. When these values are evident, choices are made without hesitation and are rarely second-guessed.

Reflections by Carol:

I have lived in every region of the country at some time in my life. I can attest to the broad generalizations cited in this chapter because I have experienced them personally. The most valuable lesson I learned along the way is that, no matter who you are, where you are from, what primary language you speak, how you were raised, or what level of education you achieved, we are all human beings trying to do and be our very best.

I have met people who are struggling to change their circumstances, to rise above and move beyond the poverty, violence, or abuse they have suffered. But regardless of their background, they all share one thing in common: hope. They may lose it for a while, and it may be hard to find, but there is always someone just around the corner to help.

My greatest lesson in powering through adversity came from a woman who worked for our company when I was in Hawaii. She came to Hawaii after after leaving Vietnam on a boat lift at the end of the War. She had lost her husband and had three young children to raise. When she arrived, she didn't speak a word of English; she was shy, scared, and penniless. The Vietnamese community embraced her, and for several years she worked menial jobs in restaurants and cleaned houses while she raised her children and worked on getting an education. It took almost ten years for her to get on her feet. Her children all went on to college, which she paid for entirely. Over the years, she chose to educate herself to earn a better living, and in time she was no longer working in a dish pantry at the back of a restaurant—she was a full-time real estate professional earning well into the six figures. She was confident and beautiful, both inside and out.

Why do I share this story? Well, living in Hawaii was a cultural shock for a white Anglo-Saxon who was raised in New Jersey. I've always said it was the closest I ever came to living in a foreign country but still being in the United States. It was by far my favorite place of everywhere I lived. I learned so much from the Hawaiian culture, along with the merging influences from our Japanese, Korean, Indonesian, Chinese, Portuguese, and Latino populations. When you live on an island 2,500 miles from anywhere else and a five-hour flight in any direction before you see land, you truly appreciate the people who live close to you.

The word for *family* in Hawaiian is "ohana." It also means "no one is left behind or forgotten." That was my experience living there; I embraced the lifestyle, and I was embraced by the people. I was inspired by the stories, many similar to my friend Linh's from Vietnam. I often wondered if the circumstances were reversed and I was the one who found myself in a foreign country, not speaking the language, with three young children to raise, and no means of support, would I be able to do it? I can't honestly answer that question because I never had to face it.

What I do know is that when we all work together sharing common core values and a commitment to protecting our families and our freedom, we will all be better people.

Reflections by Alan

I have lived in West Virginia all my life. In my younger years, a sense of wanderlust was instilled in me to see the world, and thankfully I have been able to do just that. I made a decision to visit all fifty states before I turned forty, and I did. I have also been to four of the seven continents, and I plan to visit the remaining three in the near future. As a side note, my suggestion is to write down all the places you wish to visit. Do it with pen and paper. I don't understand why, but there is something magical about writing out your thoughts by hand, as those thoughts and goals seem to come true.

My brother and I grew up in the same household with the same parents, but we have very different views on travel. I think I could be a nomad for a while and just travel the world seeing what is out there and experiencing the different cultures. My brother, who is also an engineer and has spent a great deal of time in South America and Europe for work, would rather stay home. He gets tired of business travel. He does enjoy traveling to Wyoming, Montana, and Alaska to see the wildlife because he is more of an outdoors person.

Living in West Virginia has allowed me to raise my family in a quiet, rural environment, without all the concerns a big city brings. While I will admit that West Virginia has a drug problem and crime just like any other place, it is less concentrated. During my travels, especially when I am in California (which has been quite often), my friends there always say, "I just love your accent!" And I always say, "What accent?" because I cannot hear it. However, I do have an Appalachian accent, and that probably causes some people to perceive me as being backwards. Believe me, I am not.

As I have traveled all over the world, I have learned that most everyone is the same. Nevertheless, their environment and culture heavily influences their actions and choices. Having been to Los Angeles and New York City many times, I can attest that everyone there seems to be in a hurry. As I travel further south, in rural areas—especially when we go to Myrtle Beach—the pace is much slower, and I am the one in a hurry. When I was young, I remember sitting on my grandmother's porch with many of my aunts, uncles, and cousins, just watching the world go by. Of course, those were simpler times; we only had three TV stations, a handle full of radio stations, and no cell phones, no Internet, and no email. Maybe those were the good old days after all.

One of the best lessons I learned about a person's outlook was not in the United States but in Africa. In 2010 my son Jesse and I, along with several folks from our church, went to Accra in West Africa on a mission trip to work at an orphanage. This was our first trip to Africa and Jesse's first trip out of the United States. Saying that we ran headfirst into culture shock is putting it mildly. Accra, the capital of Ghana, has a population of four million people, which is roughly comparable to the population of Los Angeles. Traffic was worse than any big city in the states, and we learned quickly that Ghana has traffic "suggestions" instead of laws. Cars legally have the right of way over pedestrians. So if you are walking, watch out!

The orphanage was a long, two-story building that housed approximately ninety boys. The building had sleeping rooms for the boys, classrooms, a kitchen, and common areas. The backyard was a big field where the kids played soccer and baseball every day. It was located about ten miles outside of Accra in a more rural area, but there were still many houses close by.

During our time there, we installed a new pump in their water well and repaired many items around the building. Two things became quite evident to both Jesse and me. These kids had nothing—by our standards, anyway. They had a few clothes, a few toys they shared among all the boys, and little else in way of material things. They did have a good roof over their heads and a group of people who loved them, and took care of them. But most of all, they had each other.

Jesse said to me, "Dad, back home, I have a TV in my room, a PlayStation, X-Box, a computer, and all the video games I've ever wanted. I never have to worry about things because you and Mom take care of Justin and me. But I see these kids here who have nothing, and they are all happy. Why is that?" Truthfully, I struggled with that answer myself. After thinking for a while and observing the kids over the next several days, I came to the conclusion that we in America have way too much. We have so many choices in almost everything that we get overwhelmed and can't make up our minds. And because we have all these choices, we want them *all*. And if we don't get them all, we are disappointed and feel we have missed out on something.

In reality we don't really need nearly as much as we have. We don't *need* all the cable channels, or XM Radio or Pandora, the fastest Internet, or that new Lexus. We just *want* them. And while there is nothing wrong with wanting, yearning to have those things, in the long run is that really what makes us happy? No, it is family and friends that really make us happy. Time spent being productive and useful, helping others, and making the world a better place is what truly stirs our soul and makes our heart sing.

The boys at this orphanage were happy because they had people who loved them, took care of them, educated them, and were helping them become all they could be. But most of all they had each other, and they just enjoyed being boys. That is what made them happy.

Maybe we should simplify our own lives and see if we are happier . . .

We are a melting pot of cultures, ethnicities, languages, education, and beliefs. In the last several decades, our population has moved from state to state and region to region. The merging of these diverse backgrounds has caused a homogenization of regional traits and characteristics. The question we should be asking ourselves is how this new mash-up of people affects the choices being made and what values are driving those choices.

Cynics would tell you that society is breaking down and our country will end up in the history books as did the Fall of the Roman Empire, the Mongol Empire, or the Russian Empire. They would argue that our values have become almost nonexistent, and the choices we are making as individuals and as a society are leading down a path of destruction. The authors of this book do not share that pessimistic view of our future. We have both traveled extensively throughout our careers and certainly have seen examples of both goodness and evil. But the goodness is always there if you just look for it. It starts with *you*. You will bring into your life what you want and expect, and if you expect the worst in people, then you will not be disappointed. Alternatively, if you expect the best, and give your best, that is what you will get in return.

Values are contagious. By examining what you truly believe and making consistent choices based on those values, you will not only attract like-minded people, you will influence others to do the same.

VALUES

*If you don't stick to your values
when they're being tested,
they're not values; they're hobbies.*
JON STEWART

THERE IS ONE undeniable truth about choices: We make better choices when our values are strong. And we make poorer choices when our values are indistinct or compromised. Sounds simple, doesn't it?

Values, however, can be equated to our lungs breathing or our hearts beating without us ever giving conscious thought to the process. When we leave the house in the morning, we don't say to ourselves, "I am going to demonstrate integrity today." When we are shopping for a pair of slacks, we don't think, "I will be honest and pay for this instead of stealing it."

Honesty and integrity are values that are either innately part of who we are or not. That's true for any values we possess. Something we were taught or discovered along the way became a key element of our very being.

What does happen as we mature is that we begin to explore and test the boundaries of our values. For example, at an early age we may witness people exhibiting their commitment to community, citizenship, and service. And then one day, we wake up with our own pledge to volunteer or serve our country . . . because those values resonate with us.

In the business world, when you see examples achievement, determination, and leadership, those individuals become our role models for how to live into the values that are blossoming within us.

If we grow up in difficult circumstances, our values are likely to be grounded in the desire for security, safety, or justice. You might be thinking that this sounds a lot like Maslow's Heirarchy of Needs.

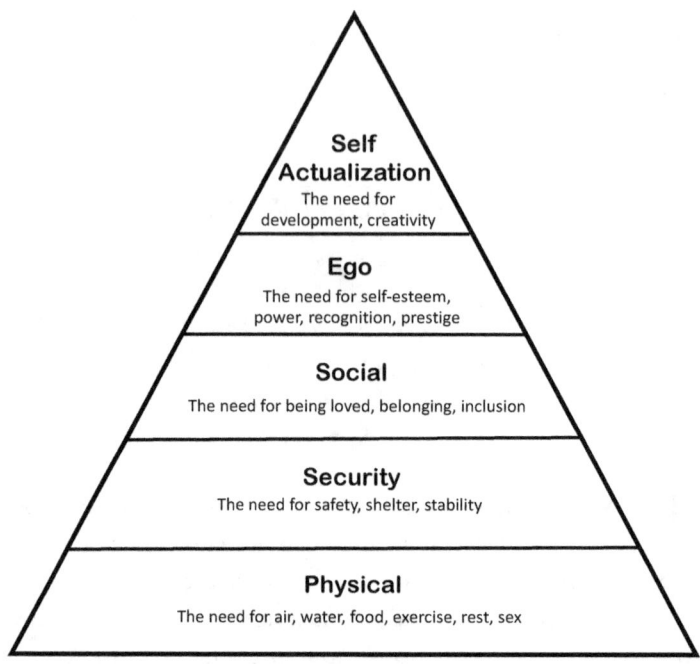

We all start at the base of the triangle at physical, then as we grow, we move up to security, then social, then ego, and finally self-actualization. Our values will manifest themselves depending on where are are in the hierarchy. If we are concerned about security, we are not tapping into values like influence or self-improvement. Likewise, if we have found our way to the top of the hierarchy, we have the freedom to explore more altruistic values such as inner harmony, peace, or spirituality.

In Maslow's theory, we all start at the bottom (babies have the most basic physiological needs) and move up the scale as we learn and grow. Circumstances may knock you back during your life, but we all have the capacity and the desire for self-actualization. But here is an interesting thought to ponder: Do the values you acquire along the way stay with you and create a compound effect, or do you exchange the values that were important early on for different values?

Let's try an experiment. Below you will see a list of values that have been amassed from a variety of experts and authorities. From this list, choose five that are most important to you today. They are listed in alphabetic order, so there is no attempt to prioritize them for you. You will find similarities in many of the words. Choose the ones that most describe the value for you.

After you have identified your *top* five, answer for yourself *why* this value is important to you and *how* it shows up in your life.

CORE VALUES

Acceptance	Family	Pleasure
Achievement	Friendships	Poise
Adventure	Fun	Popularity
Authenticity	Gratitude	Recognition
Authority	Growth	Relationships
Autonomy	Happiness	Religion
Balance	Honesty	Reputation
Beauty	Humor	Respect
Boldness	Idealism	Responsibility
Challenge	Influence	Safety
Citizenship	Inner Harmony	Security
Commitment	Integrity	Self-Discipline
Community	Justice	Self-Improvement
Compassion	Kindness	Self-Respect
Competency	Knowledge	Service
Consideration	Leadership	Spirituality
Contribution	Learning	Stability
Courage	Love	Success
Creativity	Loyalty	Status
Curiosity	Meaningful Work	Trustworthiness
Determination	Openness	Unselfishness
Fairness	Optimism	Wealth
Faith	Patience	Wisdom
Fame	Peace	Work

My Top Five Values

	Values	Why?	How does it show up in my life?
1.			
2.			
3.			
4.			
5.			

Do not agonize over words you left off your list. This doesn't mean you don't possess those values. This exercise is intended for you to get in touch with what is most important to you and explore those times when you have either demonstrated that value or it has been put to the test.

Chances are you had difficulty with this exercise, and that's OK. It shouldn't be easy, because our values are challenged every day and how we prioritize them will change over time.

It is our belief that choices we make in life are often difficult because the values underlying them are being tested. Societies over time have lived by clear values, definitive codes of conduct, and accepted morals and ethics. The consequences of violating these norms have resulted in everything from being burned at the stake and public hanging to incarceration. In modern society, violating the law can still result in incarceration, but what are the repercussions of ignoring or even trampling on core values?

Perhaps we need to take a step back and look at how values are taught in modern society. Historically, values have been instilled by parents, schools, and religious institutions. At a very early age, we teach children simple things, such as always saying please and thank you, respecting one's elders, sharing one's toys, playing fair, and being kind. But there has been a shift in our society that is contributing to what some view as a breakdown in values.

Have you ever witnessed children running around a restaurant making a scene, interrupting other patrons, and disrupting the waitstaff while their parents are engrossed in their mobile devices?

When was the last time you had a conversation with a teacher about their frustration in not being able to manage their classroom? It might have gone something like this. "I have one student who refuses to do the work in class, never completes his homework, and worse, uses loud and abusive language when speaking to me or his classmates. I used normal channels of sending letters home and after-school detention. Nothing changed, so I called for a parent-teacher conference. It was cancelled the first two times, and on the third try, the parents insisted on meeting only with the vice principal; they reported me as the problem because I was harassing their child. When I was called into the meeting, I was instructed to apologize to the parents and the student, and he was transferred to another class."

Ministers, priests, and rabbis share their concern over the dwindling population for services, Bible study, and Sunday school. One minister shared, "I worry about our children. In our community we are surrounded by teenage drug addiction and violence. And our parish is in an upscale, affluent area.

The religious leaders are working together to explore solutions for community outreach and ways to bring young families back to each of us, but it is an uphill battle when the lure of the golf course or the tennis court trumps going to church."

Reflections by Carol:

One of the people I interviewed for this book asked me a thought-provoking question: "How do you know if people are truly in touch with their values?" He told me he has discovered the answer for himself. "When I know my values are being tested, what pops into my mind is this: I couldn't live with myself if . . . I didn't take action . . . I didn't say something . . . I didn't test . . ."

We had a fascinating dialogue about this, and I would pose the same question to you. What is your answer?

Is it always necessary to make choices within the strictest interpretation of your values or is there room for compromise? And if you do compromise your values, where does it begin and where does it end? Let me share a simple example. Theft is stealing someone else's property. I would hazard a guess that there isn't a child in the universe that at some moment in time took something that didn't belong to them. It could have been a cookie from the cookie jar they weren't supposed to take unless they had permission from Mom. It could have been gum from the candy store when no one was looking. It could have been a scarf that they slipped into their purse when they were shopping because they bought this fabulous new blouse and needed but couldn't afford the scarf. It could have been in visiting someone's home or a restaurant and helping themselves to a pack of sugar or a few pills from the medicine cabinet.

Or it could have been someone's car . . . someone's jewelry—do you see where I'm going with this? Taking things that don't belong to you can become a way of life. And depending on the need and the motivation behind it, it just continues to escalate; the value of the item gets bigger and bigger, and the consequences become stronger and stronger. Where do you draw the line?

Back to that child who took a cookie from the cookie jar without Mom's permission. Even though they knew it was too close to dinner, they took it anyway. Or the child who stole the pack of gum because Mom wasn't paying attention—and what's a pack of gum anyway?

When those things are discovered and caught, how they are handled and the lessons we learn from them shape our choices and values going forward. For example, with a cookie, the child might be sent to bed without dinner.

The child is not going to die if they miss one meal. But maybe it was a meal they really like and had been looking forward to. Maybe they enjoy sitting with Mom and Dad and their siblings, and now they miss that camaraderie.

So there's a punishment, although it's mild. If a child is caught stealing pack of gum, they might take the money out of their allowance, go back to the store with Mom, tell the clerk owner what they did, apologize, and make restitution.

This reinforces right and wrong, and it demonstrates that a little bit of humiliation helps to develop humility. The child learns that there are people beyond them who matter, who have rights, feelings, and responsibilities. The child also learns that we can't make rules for ourselves. We should take into consideration how our actions affect other people. If we learn those lessons well and if they are reinforced consistently at a very young age, chances are they will stick with us into our teenage years, into adulthood, and beyond.

But let's imagine a different scene. Mom finds out about the pack of gum, tells the child he'll need to use her allowance to pay for the gum and apologize to the store clerk, and then says, "We're going to talk to your father when he comes home." But instead of agreeing with his wife, the dad says, "Oh, it was just a pack of gum. Let it go. I don't want to embarrass him." Wow! What message is the child receiving?

And while it *is* just a pack of gum, taking it without paying for it was still wrong. It's breaking the law. And the law is there so we learn to obey right from wrong.

How people who love and guide you handle situations like this is indeed important. How they deal with it develops your thinking, your beliefs, your values, and your very future. In all of our choices, we demonstrate commitment to our own values and shape the values of another generation.

There are two distinct schools of thought when it comes to values. People that are value-driven don't allow themselves any wiggle room. Their decisions and their choices tend to be black-and-white, whereas people whose values are a little cloudier, unsure, and perhaps untested will make choices at any given time based on the relative importance of that value to them and to others. You can argue that this is a rationalization: You either hold a value or you don't. Or you can take the view that values are the beacons that guide us but they are not inflexible. They aren't solid-steel rods that go from the ground to the outer reaches of the universe beyond your vision. They don't move in the wind, and for most people, this is where the conundrum lies. What are my values and how far am I willing to push or test those values?

Let's say one of your values is the value of human life and the belief that everyone is created equal and deserves the same opportunities. This value is so important to you that you've contributed to causes, you've shown up at public protests, you've written letters to your congressman, and you've preached to anyone who would listen. And then something happens; because of someone else's attitude, threat, or education, you find yourself backing away. You look at the situation and wonder, "How far would I be willing to go for this person?"

Let's make it very real. There's a homeless man in town; you've seen him from time to time. You've even dropped some coins or a bill or two to help him. And it made you feel good; it made you feel like you were honoring him as a human being and doing your part to make his life maybe just a little bit easier. And then one night this same face shows up in your home in the middle of the night as an intruder and holds a knife to the throat of one of your children. He didn't know it was your house. He didn't know you were the one who had helped him. Your neighborhood was targeted, probably somewhat randomly, your house was accessible, and he broke in because of his desperation for food and money.

In that moment how would you react? Would your respect for equality, human rights, and fair play still be the same? And would that incident color how you viewed others from that day forward? Would you stop giving contributions to the homeless? Would you stop advocating for justice? Would you channel your energies toward some other cause or some other value? It's an important societal question and one that a lot of people grapple with every day.

Think of it as the "yeah, but" syndrome. Yeah, I'll take care of him, but only under these circumstances. Yeah, I'll contribute to the cause, but only if . . ."

Are your values clear to you? Do they show up in your actions and your deeds? Are you surrounded by people who share the same values? Or are your values elastic—sometimes convenient and other times inconvenient? If you want to have faith in your ability to make the right choices for *you*, then start and end the process with your values. Every one of our contributors could identify that value or values that helped them make a life-changing choice. But where were those values when they were making less than desirable choices?

If we agree that values are learned at an early age, usually from our parents, teachers, or religious influence, then perhaps that's the first place to look. Is it fair to say that there was a time in our society when values were clearer and there was a general acceptance of right and wrong? Television is a good barometer for this assertion.

In the 1950s and 60s, we watched shows like *The Adventures of Ozzie and Harriet, Father Knows Best, Leave It to Beaver, The Brady Bunch, The Waltons, Bonanza, Gunsmoke, My Three Sons, I Love Lucy, The Andy Griffith Show*—the list goes on. Core to all these shows was that they ended with some moral or ethical lesson. Right was right and wrong was wrong, and no matter what challenges or situations occurred during an episode, it was always resolved with a positive message. Television writers and producers reflected social norms.

Fast-forward to the shows that air now. *Two Broke Girls, The Kardashians, Honey Boo Boo, The Real Housewives of (fill in the city), The Simpsons, Gossip Girl, Mad Men, Californication, King of Queens, Jackass, The Office, South Park, The Sopranos*—again the list goes on. Some of these shows are critically acclaimed and wildly popular, but what message are they communicating and leaving with viewers?

There is no question that audience tastes have changed, and the boundaries of what censors allow have expanded. If shows are viewed as farce or exaggerated reality, then we can agree that they are entertaining. But when reality in real life begins to mirror the exaggerated antics on the screen, we begin to see the deterioration of values.

The shows that have tackled contemporary issues surrounding the changing family like Will and Grace, Full House, Who's the Boss, and Modern Family all found ways to incorporate reality and humor. Each found different ways to express the values and the challenges we face in society today.

There is no simple answer to how television, movies, music, video games, and other forms of entertainment impact how we act and react in our everyday lives. But we know it does. Just turn on the news and listen for the latest report on copycat crimes mirroring an episode on TV. Listen to the language used by children, which is full of words and phrases from their favorite animation shows.

We are not suggesting that things would be different if television producers were still making shows like Ozzie and Harriet. Heaven forbid! The question we are posing is this: Are values being learned through a flat screen TV or mobile device instead of in the classroom, at the dinner table, or in Sunday School?

If values statements such as be kind to everyone, share your toys, help others in need, be a person of integrity, be courteous and respectful, always say please and thank you, learn to forgive, take responsibility, and do no harm were firmly ingrained in our children, then the effects of media (in whatever form) would be limited.

When parents, teachers, and religious leaders work together, the results are powerful. Negative role models, explicit movies, provocative music, and outrageous behaviors are neutralized. No matter how suggestive or tempting the outside influence, it is seen as purely entertainment and not a representation of how to act in the real world.

Perhaps the contemporary influences from all media sources, including the Internet, are what have contributed to the elasticity of values. It isn't that we don't have any values; instead it may be that our values are not as crystal clear and inflexible as they once were. Maybe that's good or even necessary. But we have to ask ourselves: How far will that elastic band stretch? When does compromising integrity become lack of integrity? Does trustworthiness lose meaning only when we are caught breaking the trust? Are contribution and compassion still relevant when you make a pledge—or only after you write the check?

By taking the time to assess our stated values against our actions and our words, we can begin to understand ourselves better. We learn the boundaries of the values we are willing to go to the mat for and those we will walk away from. Only you can make those decisions. Only then will you be in touch with your capacity to make better choices.

EVALUATING CHOICES

*Life is a matter of choices,
and every choice you make makes you.*
JOHN C. MAXWELL

WHAT IS THE key to making better choices? (And *better* is a qualitative word.) We believe the right choices are tied to values. Now that you have completed the Values Assessment, there is another exercise we'd like to recommend.

Write down an important choice you have made in your life—past tense—something you have already done. The category doesn't matter. Just something that stands out to you when you look back on your life. "I made a choice to do that." Here are some examples to get you thinking:

I made a choice to drop out of college.

I made a choice to change careers.

I made a choice to divorce my spouse.

I made a choice to move across the country.

I made a choice to go back to church.

Once you've picked yours, next answer some basic questions surrounding that choice. The purpose is to get clarity around what was going on in your life at the time.

Who was involved?

What were the circumstances?

Where were you?

How did you execute the choice?

How and to whom did you communicate your choice?

When did this happen?

What was the result or outcome?

After you have answered those questions, then explore the WHY.

Why was this choice so important?

Why did you make *that* choice?

What was the driving force that led you to make the choice that you made?

And finally, tap into your values. What were the values that guided and influenced you in making that choice? What were the things you would not and could not compromise in spite of other things that may have been influencing you to go a different direction?

When you complete this exercise, you should find a very clear picture of your own personal process of how you make choices—specifically regarding this choice—and truly understanding the values that are important to you.

The next exercise involves tackling a choice you are facing today. What is a choice that's sitting there, sort of rolling around like a marble on a plate? It rolls back and forth; it doesn't really tip over the edge, but it hasn't quite settled yet. The movement of that marble represents what is most likely going on in your head and your heart. *I could go this way. I could that way. I could roll back again. I could go a different direction.*

Use this exact same process. What is the situation? Define it as the choice you are facing. Then answer the questions.

When ideally should this choice be made?

What are the components of the choice before me?

What are the potential consequences?

And then go to the WHY.

Why this choice?

Why now?

Why is this important to me?

How will this choice show up in my life and reflect my values?

Go back to your list of top five values and see if they apply here. If they don't, then review the entire list and see what resonates with you. The *WHY* and your *VALUES* should be in sync for you to make a confident choice.

There are times when you will be faced with multiple choices, and if you go through this exercise, you will realize that perhaps you are agonizing over a choice that in the scheme of things isn't really that important and doesn't mean that much to you. It doesn't impact your values. It doesn't even affect your values. The choice may be about other people. It could be a throwaway choice. You just make it to be done with it. Or it could be time to defer or ignore a choice. You may find yourself thinking, "I'm putting energy into a choice that really doesn't suit my agenda or life right now. It's not going to change anything, and it's not going to move me forward. In fact, it might move me backward."

This question process we've created for helping you to analyze and make choices is something that you may or may not choose to do in print each time you are grappling with a big choice, but hopefully it will become deeply ingrained in you in terms of what will lead you to make the right choice for yourself.

These questions go beyond the information and facts in front of you at any given time and takes you to a deeper place. Choices are a part of life. We make them every day. But the big choices can have a life-changing, dramatic, and long-lasting impact on us and the people we care about. Some choices are irrevocable. Getting in touch with your values and taking the time to process making choices in a different way will manifest the results you're looking for.

LAST THOUGHTS

*If you really want to do something,
you'll find a way.
If you don't, you'll find an excuse.*
JIM ROHN

LET'S SAY THAT today was your last day on earth; when the sun came up tomorrow, you would no longer be here. What would you do?

- Would you spend more time at the office trying to finish that report or make that last sale?
- Would you skip work and spend all day with your family, your spouse, your kids, your parents, and your siblings?
- Would you call someone to mend a fence that's been broken for way too long?

What would you do if you knew that today was your last day?

To make it even more urgent, what if you only had an hour? If you knew that sixty minutes from now you would be gone, what would you do?

We are all here for a reason and a season. For some it's a very short time, and for others it may be a hundred years or more. We have no control over this, and we don't understand why. But the life we've been given is ours to own and to master.

What is most important to you in your life? We urge you to stop for a moment (or three) and think about that. If every choice you make from now on is framed with the question, "What if this is the last choice I ever get to make?" then you will *always* make the right choice.

CREDITS

*When your values are clear to you,
making decisions become easier.*
Roy E. Disney

WE ARE TRULY grateful for all our contributors during the writing of this book. For some we changed their identities to protect their privacy due to the sensitivity of their stories. The list below represents our contributors who have allowed us to use their real identity and share their contact information.

Business:
Bonnie Tyler, Creator, The Negg™
https://neggmaker.com

Environment:
Chuck Peavey, Executive Director, Business Environmental Coalition
https://Businessenvironmentalcoalition.org

Family and Friends:
Christopher Rausch, Creator of The KickAss Guide to Life
https://christopherrausch.com

Personal:
Dr. Susan L. Mowatt, MD, Inmate Care Physician
United States Penitentiary, Canaan, Waymart, Pennsylvania

Self-Discovery:
Catherine Carlisi, Carlisi Consulting Group
http://carlisigroup.com

Suicide:
Bob Donnell, CEO, Next Level Live, Inc.
https://nextlevellive.com

Education:
Hans Hanson, Founder and CEO, CollegeLogic
https://mycollegelogic.com

Career and Work:
Ken Herron, Chief Marketing Officer, Unified Inbox
https://twitter.com/kenherron
ken@kenherron.com

RECOMMENDED RESOURCES

*You are today who you'll be in
Five years except for the people
You meet and the books you read.*
CHARLIE "TREMENDOUS" JONES

THE AUTHORS ARE both avid readers and researchers. We wanted to provide additional resources covering the different aspects discussed in this book. Enjoy!

48 Days to the Work You Love: Preparing for the New Normal, by Dan Miller

50 Things to Do When You Turn 50: 50 Experts on the Subject of Turning 50, by Ronnie Sellers

60 Things to Do When You Turn 60: 60 Experts on the Subject of Turning 60, by Ronnie Sellers

70 Things to Do When You Turn 70: More Than 70 Experts on the Subject of Turning 70, by Ronnie Sellers

Adult Children of Emotionally Immature Parents: How to Heal from Distant, Rejecting, or Self-Involved Parents, by Lindsay C. Gibson

Awaken the Giant Within: How to Take Immediate Control of Your Mental, Emotional, Physical and Financial Destiny!, by Tony Robbins

Bargaining for Advantage: Negotiation Strategies for Reasonable People 2nd Edition, by G. Richard Shell

Barking Up the Wrong Tree: The Surprising Science Behind Why Everything You Know About Success is (Mostly) Wrong, by Eric Barker

Blink: The Power of Thinking Without Thinking, by Malcolm Gladwell

Boundaries: When to Say Yes, How to Say No to Take Control of Your Life, by Henry Cloud and John Townsend

Daring Greatly: How the Courage to Be Vulnerable Transforms the Way We Live, Love, Parent, and Lead, by Brene Brown

Declutter Your Mind: How to Stop Worrying, Relieve Anxiety, and Eliminate Negative Thinking, by S. J. Scott and Barrie Davenport

Designing Your Life: How to Build a Well-Lived, Joyful Life, by Bill Burnett and Dale Evans

Dinner with a Perfect Stranger: An Invitation Worth Considering, by David Gregory

Drive: The Surprising Truth About What Motivates Us, by Daniel H. Pink

Eat That Frog: 21 Great Ways to Stop Procrastinating and Get More Done in Less Time, by Brian Tracy

Emotional Intelligence 2.0:, by Travis Bradberry, PhD and Jean Greaves

Emotional Intelligence: Why It Can Matter More Than IQ, by Daniel Goleman

Enchantment: The Art of Changing Hearts, Minds, and Actions, by Guy Kawasaki

Feeling Good: The New Mood Therapy, by David D. Burns

Getting to Yes: Negotiating Agreement Without Giving In, by Roger Fisher and William L. Ury

Give and Take: Why Helping Others Drives Our Success, by Adam Grant

Grit: The Power of Passion and Perseverance, by Angela Duckworth

Holy Bible, The

How Successful People Think: Change Your Thinking, Change Your Life, by John C. Maxwell

How to Stop Worrying and Start Living, by Dale Carnegie

How to Talk So Kids Will Listen and Listen So Kids Will Talk, by Adele Faber and Elaine Mazlish

How to Win Friends and Influence People, Dale Carnegie

Influence: The Psychology of Persuasion, Revised Edition, by Robert Cialdini, PhD

Just Listen: Discover the Secret to Getting Through to Absolutely Anyone, by Mark Goulston

Lean In: Women, Work, and the Will to Lead, by Sheryl Sandberg

Living Forward: A Proven Plan to Stop Drifting and Get the Life You Want, by Michael Hyatt and Daniel Harkavy

Make Your Bed: Little Things That Can Change Your Life . . . and Maybe the World, by William H. McRaven

Man's Search for Meaning, by Viktor E. Frankl

Many Miles to Go: A Modern Parable for Business, by Brian Tracy

Mastery, by Robert Green

RECOMMENDED RESOURCES | 193

Me, Inc.: Build an Army of One, Unleash Your Inner Rock God, Win in Life and Business, by Gene Simmons

Men Are from Mars, Women Are from Venus: The Classic Guide to Understanding the Opposite Sex, by John Gray, PhD

Mindset: The New Psychology of Success, by Carol S. Dweck

Mindshift: Break Through Obstacles to Learning and Discover Your Hidden Potential, by Barbara Oakley

No Excuses!: The Power of Self-Discipline, by Brian Tracy

No Limits: Blow the CAP Off Your Capacity, by John C. Maxwell

One-Minute Millionaire: The Enlightened Way to Wealth, by Mark Victor Hansen and Robert G. Allen

Originals: How Non-Conformists Move the World, by Adam Grant

Outwitting the Devil: The Secret to Freedom and Success, by Napoleon Hill

Pre-Suasion: A Revolutionary Way to Influence and Persuade, by Robert Cialdini, PhD

Quiet: The Power of Introverts in a World That Can't Stop Talking, by Susan Cain

Rich Dad, Poor Dad: What Rich Teach Their Kids About Money That the Poor and Middle Class Do Not!, by Robert R. Kiyosaki

Rock Your Life: Encouraging Stories to Inspire and Motivate You to Rock Your Life, by Craig Duswalt

Shut Up, Stop Whining, and Get a Life: A Kick-Butt Approach to a Better Life, by Larry Winget

Stadium Status: Taking Your Business to the Big Time, by John Brubaker

Strengths Finder 2.0, by Tom Rath

Switch: How to Change Things When Change Is Hard, by Chip Heath and Dan Heath

Thanks for the Feedback: The Science and Art of Receiving Feedback Well, by Douglas Stone and Sheila Heen

The 4-Hour Work Week: Escape 9-5, Live Anywhere, and Join the New Rich, by Tim Ferris

The 7 Habits of Highly Effective People: Powerful Lessons in Personal Change, by Stephen R. Covey

The Art of Happiness: 10th Anniversary Edition: A Handbook for Living, by Dalai Lama

The Art of War, Sun Tzu

The Art of Woo: Using Strategic Persuasion to Sell Your Ideas, by G. Richard Shell and Mario Moussa

The Charge: Activating the 10 Human Drives that Make You Feel Alive, by Brendon Burchard

The Compound Effect, by Darren Hardy

The Defining Decade: Why Your Twenties Matter - And How to Make the Most of Them Now, by Meg Jay, PhD

The Four Agreements: A Practical Guide to Personal Freedom (A Toltec Wisdom Book), by Don Miguel Ruiz and Janet Mills

The Gifts of Imperfection: Let Go of Who You Think You're Supposed to Be and Embrace Who You Are, by Brene Brown

The Last Lecture, by Randy Pausch

The Leadership Moment: Nine True Stories of Triumph and Disaster and Their Lessons for Us All, by Michael Useem

The Millionaire Messenger, by Brendon Burchard

The Miracle Morning: The Not-So-Obvious Secret Guaranteed to Transform Your Life (Before 9AM), by Hal Elrod

The Noticer: Sometimes, all a person needs is a little perspective, by Andy Andres

The Power of Habit: Why We Do What We Do in Life and Business, by Charles Duhigg

The Power of Now: A Guide to Spiritual Enlightenment, by Eckhart Tolle

The Power of Positive Thinking, by Dr. Norman Vincent Peale

The Purpose Driven Life: What on Earth Am I Here For?, by Rick Warren

The Push: A Climber's Journey of Endurance, Risk, and Going Beyond Limits, by Tommy Caldwell

The Road Less Traveled, Timeless Edition: A New Psychology of Love, Traditional Values and Spiritual Growth, by M. Scott Peck, MD

The Secret, by Rhonda Byrne

The Secret Lives of Introverts: Inside Our Hidden World, by Jenn Granneman

The Seven Principles for Making Marriage Work: A Practical Guide from the Country's Foremost Relationship Expert, by John Gottman and Nan Silver

The Seven Spiritual Laws of Success: A Practical Guide to the Fulfillment of Your Dreams, by Deepak Chopra

The Success Principles™—10th Anniversary Edition: How to Get from Where You Are to Where You Want to Be, by Jack Canfield and Janet Switzer)

The Tipping Point: How Little Things Can Make a Big Difference, by Malcolm Gladwell

Think and Grow Rich: The Original, an Official Publication of the Napoleon Hill Foundation, by Napoleon Hill

Thrive: The Third Metric to Defining Success and Creating a Life of Well-Being, Wisdom, and Wonder, by Arianna Huffington

Through the Eyes of a Lion: Facing Impossible Pain, Finding Incredible Power, by Levi Lusko

Twelve Pillars, by Jim Rohn and Chris Widener

Upward Bound: Nine Original Accounts of How Business Leaders Reached Their Summits, by Michael Useem

What Every BODY Is Saying: An Ex-FBI Agent's Guide to Speed-Reading People, by Joe Navarro and Marvin Karlins, PhD

What's Wrong with Damn Near Everything!: How the Collapse of Core Values Is Destroying Us and How to Fix It, by Larry Winget

When Things Fall Apart: Heart Advice for Difficult Times (20th Anniversary Edition), by Pema Chodron

Where to Go from Here: Reinventing Your Business and Your Career, by Doug Campbell

Who Moved My Cheese?: An Amazing Way to Deal with Change in Your Work and in Your Life, by Spencer Johnson

Why Buddhism Is True: The Science and Philosophy of Meditation and Enlightenment, by Robert Wright

Will I Ever Be Good Enough?: Healing the Daughters of Narcissictic Mothers, by Dr. Karyl McBride, PhD

Wisdom Meets Passion: When Generations Collide and Collaborate, by Dan Miller and Jared Angaza

You Are a Badass: How to Stop Doubting Your Greatness and Start Living an Awesome Life, by Jen Sincero

You're Broke Because You Want to Be: How to Stop Getting By and Start Getting Ahead, by Larry Winget

Your Kids Are Your Own Fault: A Fix-the-Way-You-Parent Guide for Raising Responsible, Productive Adults, by Larry Winget

ABOUT THE AUTHORS

CAROL McMANUS is a highly sought-after speaker on subjects ranging from leadership and communication to social media and branding. The foundation from her entrepreneurial career came from years of experience living and working all over the U.S. After leaving Realogy in 2007, she established her own consulting company, and used social media to grow her business and her brand. She is the host for the wildly popular radio and podcast shows, *The LinkedIn Lady Show* and *Social Solutions*. Her unique blend of executive and life coaching along with her no-nonsense approach to personal branding have transformed companies and individuals, bringing them to new levels of success. Her success with social media led her to become an expert strategist in the field. She founded CKC Global Media to assist entrepreneurs and companies to "elevate their message and amplify their voice" using speaking, broadcasting, and publishing as a way to differentiate themselves from the competition and effectively using social media to market their message. Years of studying people and business and analyzing how and why they make the choices they do all led to the writing of this book. She is also the author of *Ten Traits for Top Performers*. Carol lives in Pennsylvania with her husband, Kevin and their Golden Retriever, Cooper.
http://ckcglobalmedia.com

ALAN SKIDMORE is a consultant and speaker. He is involved in both the technology and personal development fields, which has taken him from being an electrical engineer in the automotive industry to an IT director for a university, all while simultaneously being an international speaker, author, and radio show host. He has designed and implemented technology from automotive assembly lines and 40-gig computer networks to high-voltage substations. For over thirty years, Alan has studied personal development and read well over two thousand books, and he has become an expert in taking complex subjects and making them easier to understand. He founded Alan Skidmore International and Skidmore Technologies, where his experience and commonsense approach to life help bring simplicity and a "get-it-done" environment to companies and individuals alike. He is the host for the popular radio show *Prime Time Success with Alan Skidmore* where he shares people's stories and ideas encouraging listeners to raise their thinking and solve problems. He is also the co-author of *Rock Your Life*.
http://alanskidmore.com

www.ingramcontent.com/pod-product-compliance
Lightning Source LLC
Chambersburg PA
CBHW071614080526
44588CB00010B/1124